JULIE SAMUEL

What Are We Going To Do About *Julie?*

novum pro

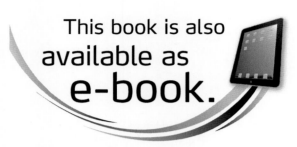

This book is also available as e-book.

w w w . n o v u m - p u b l i s h i n g . c o . u k

© 2023 novum publishing

ISBN 978-3-99131-819-4
Editing: Charlotte Middleton
Cover photos: Julie Samuel
Cover design, layout & typesetting:
novum publishing
Internal illustrations:
see bibliography p. 125.

The images provided by the author
have been printed in the highest
possible quality.

www.novum-publishing.co.uk

Climate neutral
Print product
ClimatePartner.com/16547-2201-1002

IN THE BEGINNING

In the early years, your basic character is formed. Parental influence, sibling behaviour and friendships can affect how you interact with others and help to shape your judgement of what is good and what is bad. I was born six weeks premature in Highgate Nursing Home on the 15th May 1944 and my poor mother was warned that I was unlikely to survive the night.

I am the youngest of four children, with two sisters (Tina, the oldest and Margaret, the second child) and a brother, Bill. I was not expected to live because I was underweight and very small. It was war time and there were few modern facilities available to cope with early births. I was born without nails or hair and was wrapped in cotton wool and placed in front of the fire at home for warmth. With my mother's care and determination, I survived. My parents were 'middle class'. My mother was the eldest daughter of William Foyle, a larger-than-life entrepreneur who, from a barrow selling second-hand books, became the greatest book shop owner in the world. But this was war time and times were hard. Our mother would queue outside the local butcher's shop to buy a small amount of meat or offal to feed her family of five, whilst my father was away, serving in the army in Egypt.

We lived in a suburban house in leafy Surrey, having moved there before World War Two. It appeared to us that we were indeed very fortunate, for, although both our parents worked, our grandfather was always there to see that we never starved or went without essential goods, and our mother would come home from London with a leg of lamb or beef which my grandmother had managed to get from local farmers. But there is more to say about my grandparents later.

Samuel Family

I was three when I first met my father. At that time, he was a stranger to me. The separation by war had affected everyone, especially the women, who were running the household until, suddenly, the fathers turned up and started to interfere with routines. I think my father felt useless, as his role in the army was now over, and he had to find another position as the man of the house.

He too was an entrepreneur. I remember that one day he decided to raise chickens. The very next day a box arrived packed with day-old chicks. Then, overnight, we lost some, which drowned in their water bath. So, he decided to put the remaining chicks outside in a makeshift pen in the garden. We then lost a few more of them to foxes and other predators! I have always loved animals and longed for pets of my own.

My mother was not overly protective and allowed me to play in the chicken run. She gave me a pudding basin, a wooden spoon and watering can and left me to play mud pies. I soon started to train the chickens and, having been to a circus, could see myself performing with my troop of colourful hens.

First, I had them jumping over logs. This wasn't easy, but with a little push they eventually got the hang of it and, rather than face me, leapt over, flapping and squawking furiously. I soon realised that they just didn't have the brain power to take orders, so my ambition came to an end.

Our garden was typical of the 1930s style, with a neat lawn, borders, and a vegetable patch at the bottom. It backed on to a wonderful wood and heathland called Borough Heath, an amazing place for children to have as a wild playground. We went there often, taking a picnic and spending all day climbing trees and making camps out of branches and heather. There was a large pond in the middle of the heath that sometimes iced over in the winter, and we would slide across it and revel in falling over. Once, when I was playing there with friends, I fell out of a tree and knocked myself out. My friends were worried about me, as I briefly lost my memory. They decided that I must not go home until I knew my name and where I was from, as they thought we would all get into trouble. Thankfully the concussion didn't last, and I was able to act normally and pretend nothing had happened. Our house also had a small crazy-paved terrace outside the French windows from the lounge.

Our parents sometimes left us on our own, unchaperoned, as was fairly usual in those days; nobody thought anything of it. My siblings used this time to have fun with me in a rather sadistic way. I adored my brother Bill, as he was a kind and caring boy, and I always stood up for him. In fact, I still feel very protective of him today. Well, my sisters, and our next-door neighbour, Josephine, who spent most of her childhood in our house, decided to play hospitals and doctors. They used Bill as the patient, and Josephine would dress up as a stranger, say she was a doctor and knock on the door and ask to examine Bill. Then she would announce that she would have to amputate a limb. So, out would come an axe and some knives (health and safety regulations didn't exist in those days), and they would lay him on the dining room table with a sheet over him and make me listen behind the door as they supposedly hacked away at a leg or an arm, while I screamed and begged them to stop. When they had had enough of me, they just locked me out of the house in the back garden and laughed and made faces at me through the French windows.

One day I got so mad, I dragged the heavy wooden garden broom over and smashed it through the window, which shattered into shards of glass and went all over my tormentors. Life stood still at that moment as I relished the fearful looks on their faces. They had it coming!

I commandeered that broom as my own personal weapon. I was often bullied by a local boy in the street. He would ride his bike at high speed then slam the brakes on just before he hit me. I forged a plan and dragged my weapon (the faithful garden broom) to the front of our drive and lay in wait for him to come speeding down the street. I hid behind the flowering cherry tree, the broom resting behind me. Of course, timing was everything, as I couldn't attempt this assault twice.

Suddenly, there he was, almost up to me. I crouched down, ready for the kill, and up I came, wielding the broom through the air, aiming it straight at him and knocking him right off his bike. I didn't wait to see the damage; I just legged it back to the house and pretended to be playing quietly. Around six o'clock there was a knock on the front door. I watched as my mother, wiping her hands on her pinafore, opened it to see who it was. The boy was standing next to a large, rotund woman. I could see the blood-stained bandage on his head and his red, tear-stained face.

"Mrs Samuel," she said, "your daughter has caused a terrible injury to my son."

Straight away my mother asked, "Which daughter was it? I have three." When the woman replied with my name, pointing an accusing finger at me while I hid behind my mother, my mother simply said, "What? You mean your twelve-year-old son can't defend himself against my five-year-old daughter? Well, I suggest you send him to a boxing class! Goodbye." And she closed the door firmly. Mysteriously, the broom disappeared, and the boy stayed well clear of me after that. I would never condone using this method for protection or revenge but being a vulnerable five-year-old, I taught myself how to fight back against bullies.

Our parents had a volatile relationship, with vicious rows fuelled by alcohol. We would sit on the stairs behind the bannisters, listening to the insults and threats. This was very worrying, as we were never sure that it wouldn't end in a physical fight. Then the next day they would carry on as though nothing had happened. I suppose you get used to anything if it becomes a regular occurrence, hence the number of badly abused children who continue to love their parents. We loved them both in different ways.

In order for my parents to carry on working, my mother hired a number of mothers' helps to look after us while she went to work. Later, she employed girls from the continent. She also employed au pairs here in England to learn English and do some child-minding and housework.

My father always had an eye for an attractive female and one night, after a session at the local pub, got out of bed to visit the toilet. Having finished what he went in to do, he came out and instead of turning right, turned left into an au pair's room and got into bed with her. There was a lot of squealing and commotion coming from her room until my mother arrived and directed him back to bed. Another night, my father came out of the toilet and went straight ahead, tumbled over the bannisters and rolled down the stairs, but we all know how drunkards feel no pain!

My mother was very well-educated and spoke French and German, having been to school in Switzerland as a teenager. She was the first person to go to when times were bad, for a cuddle, a reassuring smile and words of wisdom. She was the opposite of my father: kind, loyal, loving and trustworthy. We all adored her, and I miss her terribly even now, although I think she keeps an eye on us from above!

My father, Edgar Samuel: saint, or sinner? He came from a theatrical family in Brixton, where many Musical Hall artists lived. His father, Horace Samuel, died very young, having contracted Spanish flu during the pandemic at the end of World War One. Before that war, he had achieved a lot in his theatrical life, first as a member of Charlie Chaplin's troupe at the Hackney Empire, then as a double act with his wife, Dorothy. He became an actor-manager and toured Europe extensively. His father was a talented artist. We don't know much about our paternal grandmother except that she was probably Irish, Dorothy O'Dell, an actress in light entertainment, who sadly died of cancer around 1948.

I cannot say that my father was anti-Semitic, but I do remember him prefixing a Jew with the adjective "bloody", which always seemed to me to be strange, coming from a person whose name was Samuel! Back in the 1900s, my grandfather had changed his name to Lawson, presuming, he thought his name, Horace Samuel, may put off people in the entertainment business and dissuade them from employing him. Along with his wife, Dorothy, the acting/singing duo became known as "Lawson & O'Dell".

Looking back over the last hundred years of entertainment, I think we will find that Jewish people dominated in the entertainment industry. Familiar names were Levi, the Cohen Brothers, Harry Saltzman (a "Bond" film producer), Goldwyn Mayer and Harvey Weinstein! Let us not forget the amazing Jewish songwriters Irving Berlin, George Gershwin and Oscar Hammerstein.

As a family, we all thought that we must have some Jewish blood, until my nephew Simon traced the Samuel family back to the early 1800s, only to find they had all been christened, married, and buried in Christian churches. Quite recently, I did a DNA test, only to find that I am indeed eight percent Ashkenazi Jew from Eastern Europe. Learning this, I then recalled that my grandfather, William Foyle, was born to an immigrant woman, and her name was Levine. His father brought his children up as Christians (as were we), and our grandmother was a Scottish Christian, whose family name was Tulloch, way back in 1680. We discovered that two of her ancestors, Barbara and her daughter, Ellen, were sentenced to death for witchcraft and hanged at the top of Gallows Hill then there were burned nearby on a large bed of peat. Their ashes are kept in a dish in the local museum of Shetland.

Dad was a frustrated man, unable to keep up in the entertainment business due to being weakened by tuberculosis in his early twenties. This was to plague him for the rest of his life, not helped by the sixty cigarettes he smoked daily. Had he been in good health and followed in his parents' footsteps, I am sure he would have been a successful actor, as he was a natural entertainer and regaled us with wonderful old music hall jokes and songs. However, he got a job at Foyles as a bookseller, and it was there that he met my mother.

My father had all the vices, smoking, drinking, gambling, and womanising, to which my mother appeared to have turned a blind eye.

I don't believe in organised religion but do find people who follow a religious lifestyle happier, more at peace, and generally wanting to help others. I don't agree with wealthy TV evangelists that money and power can change a person, as I found out later in life.

As a small child, I had a spiritual experience that made me feel there was someone watching over me. I always had a terrible fear of the dark but for no apparent reason. As soon as the lights went out, I would start to feel fear, even though I usually slept with either Tina or Margaret, my sisters. Regardless, once it was dark, I still suffered this paralysing fear and would get to a stage where I could stand it no longer and would call out to my parents, "Mum, Dad." Eventually, the hall light would go on and one of them would be in the room to comfort me, Sometimes, if I was sweating badly and with my heart pounding, they would even let me into their bed. What a relief that was. Then, one night, when I was a bit older and on my own, my sisters having gone to boarding school, I felt this creeping feeling coming up and over my body. Even though I was now older, I had to rely on myself to overcome this terrible physical feeling, so, I prayed, "Please, God, take away my fear." The prayer didn't appear to work. Then, just as I thought my heart would burst, I felt two warm hands clasp me around my face and lift me up out of bed. I looked down on my own body and felt a comforting warmth surround me in the room.

I had no reason to feel scared anymore, even though I was alone, and nothing had changed. Gradually, I returned into my body, feeling peaceful and sleepy. I have no idea what happened. All I can say is, this did happen, and I remember it vividly to this day.

Our parents often went to the pub in the evening, leaving us at home. One night, we decided to play a prank on them. My mother had a full-size tailor's dummy, as she was a great seamstress and made lots of her own clothes. Bill positioned the dummy just inside the front door and dressed it in a trench coat, topped off with a trilby hat and some dark glasses. He then tucked a full-length air rifle under the dummy's arm, pointing the rifle at the front door. We all waited, stifling giggles quietly behind the banisters, until we heard the key in the door. Suddenly, there was a scream. The dog ran downstairs barking furiously, the cat shot up the stairs, and finally our parents came in, having realised what we had done. We expected a terrible response, but they were laughing with relief and took the joke very well.

HOLIDAYS WITH THE GRANDPARENTS AT BEELEIGH ABBEY

Beeleigh Abbey

It would be remiss to leave out the times we spent with our beloved grandfather, William Foyle. There is already enough information on his life and achievements and the building of the most iconic and greatest book shop in the world, but I shall tell you about the side we all knew and loved as his grandchildren. I can only write about my own knowledge and memories of William (he didn't allow us to call him "Grandad"), but all my life I have been attracted to eccentric people, and maybe that's because of the lasting impression, and the wonderful colourful character, of William that set the bar. He was a jolly Father Christmas kind of man with shoulder-length hair and a smile always playing on his face. He smoked everything, mostly cigars, an occasional pipe and cigarettes in between, but he always smelled delicious, as he splashed liberal amounts of eau de cologne about his person, bottles of which he had placed in all his guest rooms.

My grandparents lived in an eleventh-century abbey in Beeleigh, a small hamlet near Maldon, Essex. We spent two or three weeks every summer staying with them, mostly without our parents. Our cousin, Christopher Foyle, would often stay alongside us too.

The abbey had such a rich history, having been inhabited by monks for centuries. Although when we were there it was full of laughter, it certainly had an eerie atmosphere. There were five bedrooms on the first floor and three on the second floor. We slept mostly on the top floor. All the major bedrooms had four-poster beds and were full of antique furniture, as, indeed, was the whole building. One bedroom on the third floor was named the "James Room".

Julie and Christopher James Room

The bed in there had a carving on the bedhead of James II. This room was rumoured to be haunted, but by whom, we never knew! Up against one wall was a beamed bench which had indents, grooves worn down by the monks when they said their prayers. It was thought too that the monks were made to kneel flat against the wall in penance for their sins. We were all too scared to go into that room alone, but many times one of my siblings would plot to shut one of us in there for fun. Poor Christopher; we were not very kind to him. He was outnumbered by Samuels. Once too, we trapped an exchange student from France in the room because he was most annoying and we did it to teach him a lesson, just for being French.

In the attic, William had built at waist level a huge steam-train set. There were stations, farms and all sorts of other things going on around the track. The Hornby trains were larger than normal and there was a lot of methylated spirits involved that were so highly flammable that sometimes a small fire would break out. William, who wore white cotton gloves when playing at trains, would put out the fires, but you can imagine the damage had there been a fire in this building built from ancient wood timbers.

William, though, was fearless. Later, after my grandfather died and my grandmother became frail, my aunt Christina moved into the abbey with her husband, Ron. For some unknown reason, she slept in the James Room while her bedroom was being renovated. According to her story, she awoke in the night to some violent shaking of the bed and bedside table and later found a bite on a finger, which became infected. Eventually, she was admitted to a hospital for tropical diseases, and a diphtheria germ was found that had not been seen for over one hundred years.

William took great delight in turning our beds into apple pie beds and filled them with all sorts of household items. Sometimes, a whole set of saucepans had to be removed before we could get in. As usual when younger, I suffered many sleepless nights, sleeping in a bed at the bottom of my sisters' grand four-poster, waiting for some terrible ghoul to creep in to taunt me. The days, however, were filled with the most fantastic adventures and games.

William was an avid reader and very knowledgeable about a great number of subjects. Over the years, he collected many rare books and built up a renowned library. All his books were available to us. We were encouraged to read, and I clearly remember lying in bed, looking at anatomy pictures in an enormous book probably a couple of hundred years old. Nothing in the abbey was out of bounds, even the wonderful old organ in the chapel. It was fun to play "Chopsticks" on its ivory keyboard, despite the fact it was, allegedly, the instrument on which the composer, Handel, composed his famous "Largo".

Our grandparents loved animals, as we did, and had a large overfed silver-grey Persian cat called Winston, which William carried around like a baby. The cat was a devil and loved to pick off the white doves that lived in the dovecote, but William adored him as much as he did his snappy Cairn terrier called Jock.

William sometimes took us fishing at Beeleigh Falls, a lock about twenty minutes' walk away. Whenever we went for walks, we had to choose a walking stick, some of which had Swiss badges up the front. We must have looked like a strange band of children, led by an elderly gentleman in a cream linen jacket and a Panama hat, carrying various fishing rods and boxes full of rolled up bits of dough, which we used as bait. I don't remember ever catching a fish, but I do remember we got into trouble for encouraging the French student to dive into the lock; more fool him.

On certain days of the week, the abbey was open to visitors, half a crown on the door. We, as family, were dispersed amongst the crowd as floorwalkers (people who watch out for shoplifters). This was a job we took very seriously. The French student went right over the top with a Sherlock Holmes hat and a magnifying glass. We had to also pretend we had never been around the abbey before and "ooh" and "aah" just like the real visitors. There were some amazing paintings by Turner and Constable in the abbey and a large still life by Tintoretto. When my grandfather died we were able to choose some artefacts from the abbey, and I chose a painting by Constable, *Moon Over the Yare*. It was placed on the staircase amongst many named artists, a typical rural landscape. I hoped that this eventually would be my pension. However, when I had it valued, I was told it was not genuine and was probably painted by one of John Constable's students.

Grandad with visitors

William once said, "If you want to succeed in business and not go bankrupt, don't expand until you have to ..." Wise words.

There were some old barns and fields in the grounds, and a retired racehorse called Misty. I had my first ever ride on Misty when my sisters plonked me onto his back with no saddle or bridle and chased him round the field shouting, "Hang on to his mane, then duck!" when he cantered under the trees to try and knock me off.

We had a lot of accidents during play. My sister Margaret started a course in karate and one afternoon practised some moves on Bill. He managed to throw her over his shoulder (some feat, as she was a strapping girl for her age), and unfortunately she broke her neck and ended up in hospital. For some strange reason, she was put in a geriatric ward, with people popping off from time to time. One old lady, she told us, sang the whole of Psalm 23, "The Lord Is My Shepherd", sat bolt upright, and, as the extra nod to our Lord had knocked the life out of her, then fell back dead. She would, most definitely, have been welcomed at the pearly gates.

At Beeleigh we had to dress for dinner, and Granny was very strict about manners and tradition. William would bang the gong at six thirty p.m., then serve drinks from a little corner bar he had set up in the small sitting and dining room, which was used for informal meals. He always changed for dinner into a brocade smoking jacket and a fez and pretended to pour us grown-up drinks like whisky and soda, gin and tonic, and dry martini, all in those miniature glasses that you find in charity shops; God knows what they were really meant for. I suspect they were possibly for liqueurs or, most likely, eye baths. William spent most mealtimes playing tricks with teaspoons that had holes in them, and other tricks that he had bought, out of a large "trick drawer" in the hall. We always ended the meal with cheese. His favourite was gorgonzola, and he would enjoy slipping a piece onto our plates, as we thought the smell was appalling. Once, he put some under a microscope to show us just how riddled it was with bacteria. He would also switch off his hearing aid if Granny started reprimanding him.

Sometimes, we went to Southend for the day and would go the amusement park, the Kursaal, and play on the rides. William would give us half a crown each to spend in Woolworths, we would then walk by the sea, and he would stop at a winkle and whelk stall. For lunch, we would join Granny in a hotel after she had spent the morning shopping. One day it was her birthday. I remember everyone had bought her a little gift, except me. I was very young and felt devastated I had not got something for her. So, I skipped to the hotel public toilet and used some of my pocket money to pop into a machine and delivered her a nice, brand-new sanitary towel. It was no surprise that this was not appreciated and there was an embarrassing silence. Granny was such a prude that there was never any mention of bottoms, or other body parts. It was even rumoured that when she gave birth to our mother, she thought the baby would exit through her belly button. The nurse enlightened her by saying the baby would come out the same way it went in.

Granny was the opposite of William. She was very strict and religious and tended to behave like Queen Victoria, but she was also very kind, and used to send us girls bundles of dresses that she bought in markets. She lived well into her nineties without any real health problems. She took up drinking copious amounts of champagne after my grandfather died, and for some reason accused Mr Kwey, the gardener of thirty years, of exposing himself to her. He must have been in his sixties at the time and an unlikely candidate for such a display.

Probably, because of the drink, she had a couple of falls, and when she was in her nineties she broke her hip. The doctor who examined her found a cancerous growth on her breast, which she claimed she had had for thirty years. It certainly didn't kill her, as she died quietly in her sleep aged ninety-six.

EARLY SCHOOL DAYS 1948-1956

I look back on my first school as quite a shocking experience. It was a local village primary school, founded way before we were all propped up by the National Health Service and unemployment benefits. Some of the children were filthy dirty and covered in scabies, sores and scabs and obviously not getting enough nutrition to keep them healthy. It was probably the free third of a pint of daily milk given to all young school children that saved them. Poverty was very visible in those days, and we saw many beggars on the streets, unlike today when we have so much more help for people less fortunate than us.

I wasn't at that local school for very long before my parents decided that, for them to keep working, and for us all to get a proper education, it would be best to pack us all off to boarding school. I was sent to a small mixed boarding school where they had children from various embassies, so communication could be difficult. I can't say that it was awful, but at the age of six, and still wetting the bed, it was a miserable first term. I had to wash my own sheets and hang them up in shame.

Our matron Miss Young insisted that all the juniors were to sit on chamber pots in the large reception hall and remain there until they had done a number two! I was usually the last child to perform. Paralysed by embarrassment, I would be surrounded by a sea of foul-smelling excrement until I was eventually successful!

It was a fascinating opportunity to meet so many children from different parts of the world. Banky Foster was from Africa, and I had a crush on him. I told my mother he had such a beautiful smile, just like the image of the boy on a jam jar. The "woke society" would have a shock now if a child said such a thing, but I meant it as a huge compliment. I learnt to ride ponies, something we all had to do, as my father, having been trained by the army, was a great horseman. I liked animals but found the whole horse-riding culture utterly boring and ended up trailing along at the back, singing songs to my gentle pony which, like me, seemed quite happy not to be part of the crowd.

THE GREAT ESCAPE

At the age of seven, I had had enough and planned an escape from boarding school. I had made friends with a Pakistani girl called Fakria Alisha. Where is she now, I wonder? I told my classmates I was going to run away. They laughed and said I wouldn't dare do it. That was to be a red rag to a bull, and I am convinced it was at this point that I began to feel that thrill of being a bit of a daredevil, a rebel. Fakria very kindly, but reluctantly, said she would come with me.

We also took with us the school dog, an eager mongrel, which was more than happy to join us in this expedition, as he followed us out of the building and made his own dash for freedom. We left just before morning prayers and assembly, to give us time to get away when everyone was in the main hall, paying attention. It is hard to explain the exhilarating feeling of freedom I felt, walking down the Brighton Road like a normal person instead of being a prisoner in an institution.

Horley to Tadworth was sixteen miles, quite a distance for a couple of seven-year-olds. Along the way, we were stopped by a police car.

"Where are you going, my dear?" said the kindly policeman.

"Oh, to visit my auntie," I lied. I had to lie, otherwise we would have gone that far for nothing. Surely, he must have thought it a bit odd, two small girls in school uniform, one an Asian girl, and both accompanied by a dog. Means of communication in the police force wasn't as good in those days.

At last, we crossed over the road into Shelvers Way in Tadworth, turned right into Vernon Walk and arrived home about three. My parents were at work, but fortunately, my kindly Irish neighbours, Mr and Mrs Green, took us in and cooked us a full English breakfast. Glad to be among friends, we relaxed. Not many people had cars in those days, so when I heard a car, I recognised the headmaster's Bentley coming down the road. We hid under the table when the doorbell rang, but my new friend, the trusty school mongrel, barked loudly and then ran out to greet his old owner and we were driven back to school.

The trouble I was in after that escapade was not nearly as bad as I thought it might be. My parents came down to visit, Mummy in tears and Father puffing away nervously on a cigarette as usual. They sat silently and waited for an explanation. "Well, I am very unhappy and hate boarding school," was my response. Not much of an excuse. Perhaps I should have found a shocking reason, like being beaten and abused by the lesbian games mistress. That was true, but who would believe me? Anyway, child abuse in the 1950s didn't appear to exist like it does today, well, not publicly, for what a palaver that would have caused, or perhaps it would just have been brushed under the carpet.

ST MICHAEL'S AND ST AGNES' CONVENT

My sisters, Tina and Margaret, were at this time at St Michael's and St Agnes' Anglican Convent for girls, and it was decided to send me there to be with them. Chopping and changing schools had an unsettling effect on my education. Did I think it would be any better than the last school? If so, I was in for shock. There was no capital punishment, unlike at High Trees. Physical harm was not allowed, but the punishments were still as harsh. Intimidation by a tall woman in a strange black-and-white habit was quite terrifying. I was subjected to ridicule for my lack of education and became so self-conscious of my limitations that I put on paper the very smallest amount of written work I could just about get away with. A few people at this point mentioned "Class Clown". I instinctively felt I could avoid trouble by being funny and felt it was also the only way I could detract from my dismal schoolwork.

Dyslexia wasn't widely known in the 1950s, so the only diagnosis for my ignorance was "dim". I had some very nice friends who weren't quite as naughty as I was but who appreciated my audacity and bravado. Christine Aldiss, Pattie Boyd (yes, *the* Pattie Boyd) and Angela Bailes were all good friends. Pattie and Christine were older than me and in a higher class, but we still hung out together. I got to know Pattie when we were in the sick bay together, both of us sick with scarlet fever. I was eleven years old then and had discovered pop music. Together, we sent off for signed pictures of movie stars and pop stars. Surprisingly, Pattie taught me all there was to know about sex. God only knows where she learnt it.

Christine, Patty, Charlie, Penny

I have a theory about child abuse and paedophiles. In the 1950s and 1960s we never heard about, or read about, such crimes in detail, until much later and following the Moors murders. In general, there wasn't much reported in the news or on TV. So, at that time, if a person harboured thoughts about having a sexual relationship with children, or worse, they would probably keep it to themselves, for other people would deem that to be evil and perverted. Because of public revulsion, that person would be more likely to resort to something tamer, like flashing (which happened to me numerous times). Now that we read and hear about child molestation on a frequent basis, and with the sharing of information on the internet, etcetera, a perpetrator knows it is not just him or her with twisted desires, but that there are also many thousands with similar appetites, thus encouraging the sharing of obscene material, and the belief that he or she is not so perverted after all. Maybe, if we had continued in a Victorian manner, respected common decency, and kept unpleasant practices hidden from the public, we might have fewer paedophiles.

During my time at the convent, you would think I would have been indoctrinated by ritualistic and organised religion, but that never happened. In fact, I quite enjoyed the drama, singing and chanting in chapel and did pray quite a lot. I gazed at flickering candles until I was mesmerised, thinking in my head, "So, God or Jesus, flicker once if you agree with me, and twice if not!"

We had to go into retreat once a year, which was quite a pleasant experience. You were not allowed to speak, so that restriction always caused a great deal of repressed giggling. For some reason, the food was better, and the iced buns and reading of parables and religious scripture was quite comforting. I still like to visit churches and, in stressful situations, have even written out a prayer for the priests to pray on my behalf, placing it in a little prayer box in St George's Chapel in Windsor Castle so at least I feel I'm doing something helpful regarding a solution.

One Christmas, our Aunty Chrissy (Christina Foyle) took us to the London Palladium to see the pantomime *Cinderella*. I had never been to the theatre, and this was my first experience. The lights and music were thrilling, and the costumes were fantastic. I loved it all and felt a tingling sensation that this could be something I could do. Later, I pestered my parents with questions of how I could get up on that stage and be a member of that wonderful, exclusive club.

I finally decided I would follow in my paternal grandparents' footsteps and go on the stage, encouraged by our school elocution and drama teacher, Miss Webster. She was a rotund lady with a small Pekinese dog that she carried around like some cute accessory. Miss Webster entered me for all the LAMDA Drama and Elocution exams. I came through them with flying colours and got a distinction and honours in most of them. At last, I had discovered something I was good at, a legitimate form of showing off, I suppose. We often put on plays at the convent and l loved taking part. I played Dopey in *Snow White and the Seven Dwarfs* and so enjoyed the laughter that I gradually built up my part with extra gags and pratfalls, until I was upstaging all the other dwarfs. They were so surprised at my antics they would forget their lines and "corpse" (a term for laughing on stage or on camera).

photo of Christina Foyle

When boys and girls reach puberty, they have an increased awareness of the opposite sex; it's human nature – you can't stop it. There was a new laundry being built at the back of the school, and through the bathroom window I spotted Stanley (a builder's apprentice): tall, dark and handsome. I had kissed a boy once during the school holidays. His name was Max Redpath, and he was a local boy. We saw each other for about a week (a long relationship in those days). Max wrote me a letter at school, which I passed around for everyone to read and which caused some jealousy and made me some enemies.

Anyway, Stanley wrote me a note and pushed it through the fence that separated us, rather like Pyramus and Thisbe. I cannot remember what he wrote, but I can remember the thrill and excitement to think he had chosen me to contact. I caught sight of him out of the bathroom window and waved in a regal way.

I then went about composing a reply and writing it on my best pink stationery, thus leaving evidence of my carnal sin on paper, discarding as I went letters that I felt did not come up to scratch. I should have known better, for those cunning nuns would find the notes and finally have an excuse to expel me.

We were due to have our half-term break, and I was going to Christine Aldiss' hotel, the White Heart, in Reigate. I had just returned from the record store, where I had purchased "Why Do Fools fall In Love" by Frankie Lymon and the Teenagers. I had a wind-up record player which I took to school and practically everywhere else I went. Many of my records came from Foyles bookshop, where they had a record department on the second floor. Poor Mummy was given a list of all the Brunswick and London labels and 78s, mostly American music. Rock-and-roll had not yet been taken up by our young musicians; that happened later when Lonnie Donegan started playing country rock, then Cliff Richard came along.

I am not an expert in the history of pop music but I know how much I still love it.

Mrs Aldiss had just come off the phone to my mother. She had received a call from Sister Mildred that both Christine and I were to be expelled and citing our disruptive behaviour as the reason. I later learned that Mrs Aldiss, a good Catholic, remonstrated with Sister Mildred, making threats about the refund of fees and of reporting her to the bishop, pope, etcetera, and finally managed to persuade her not to expel Christine. But it was final regarding me. There was no going back. Funnily enough, I felt no remorse or shame, just elated that I would never have to go back. I would miss my friends, for sure, but there would always be new, and exciting, horizons ahead.

What joy – a whole half-term at home and not at school! My only regret was that I had been cast to play the Pied Piper in *The Pied Piper of Hamelin*. Oh, well. At least I was moving forward toward my goal.

Secretly, I think my parents liked having me at home. They were very worldly and didn't appear to be too concerned about my disgrace. I did lots of dog walking and helping around the house and got to appreciate my parents more, as I was without my siblings and so had them to myself. Also, they seemed to be getting on better then.

Julie with Jacky dog

I think I had a special relationship with my father, having left boarding school so young and getting to know them better as people, accepting my father's shortcomings and learning to be a great deal more diplomatic with both parents and not so judgemental.

During my break from school, I started to meet local children at a gym club to which my mother sent me to get some exercise. Frankie Picket was the coolest girl ever. She lived on a council estate in Sutton with her mother and grandmother. A father was never mentioned, and her mother and grandmother were both homeworkers and beavered away making make-up bags. Frankie was a free spirit, like me, and was madly in love with Elvis Presley. Elvis was a bit too scary for me, as I must have recognised his sexual power and I was still a little too young to be interested. Tommy Steele was my pin-up idol, and Frankie and I chain-stitched their names on the backs of our jeans. It was a long, hot summer of swimming and Sunday afternoons at the cinema, "the pictures". My main mission, at the ages of twelve and thirteen, was to get out of the house without being missed. My parents weren't overly protective, but we had to be back before dark. Any time after that would cause a row.

By 1955, pop music was now geared toward teenagers. We bought many records and Frankie and I learned to jive together. She was dark and stunning, like a gypsy. She taught me to smoke, and I must have loved her lots, as she is entered in my address book as "Darling Frankie". We bought Rimmel make-up from Woolworths: pale lips and loads of eyeliner and mascara. We bought and wore push-up bras from M&S, not that we had anything there to push up, as we were only size 32 A cup. But to us, she was Gina Lollobrigida, and I was Sandra Dee, although later I decided Bridget Bardot was cooler and more my style.

1956 ITALIA CONTI

Summer was over and it was time to think about school again. It had been decided that for me to continue my education, I would go to school in Soho, London, around the corner from where my parents worked. That way, they could keep a close eye on me and, even better, it was a stage school. Hoorah! The famous Italia Conti stage school. What a blessed result. I did, of course, have to pass an audition for singing and acting. That was easy, as I had been well trained at speech and drama and had audition pieces ready. I chose a monologue spoken by Puck from *A Midsummer Night's Dream*, a piece that has stayed with me forever. Singing was a minor problem, but I could sing in tune, and I sang my version of "How Much is That Doggy in the Window" and "O Little Town of Bethlehem". I noticed a little smirk appear on Miss Conti's lips but I must have pleased them, as I got in and started the following term.

September. Shopping for stage school clothes was fascinating. We headed off with the list to Anello and Davide and Freed, well-known theatrical clothing and shoe shops stocking figure-hugging leotards, pink and black tights, fishnet tights, ballet, tap and character shoes and point blocks for classical ballet. How exotic it all seemed, and moreover, I was joining this exclusive club. We wore our own clothes between classes and could wear anything, within reason.

When I arrived on the first day, I immediately became friends with another newcomer, Sandra Bryant, a very attractive freckled-faced girl with a bubbly personality. Later, she moved to the Corona Academy stage school. I wonder what happened to her. Another girl I was friends with was Jill Gascoine, who later changed her name to Jill Mai Meredith, as there was already an actress called Gascoigne. She was petite and pretty and a good actress but a hopeless singer. Later, Jill became Michael Winner's young girlfriend and was given the part of Yum Yum in one of his early films, *The Cool Mikado*, which was a modern adaptation of the Gilbert and Sullivan classic *The Mikado*. I went to see it with my friend Liz, and we laughed aloud when she appeared singing soprano in an aria whilst walking round a swimming pool. She was obviously miming to the sound of a professional opera singer. I often wonder what happened to her too. I had dinner with Michael Winner once and he was the perfect gentleman. I felt sorry for him, because he was no oil painting and eventually became overweight and vulgar.

I was frequently given Cockney parts to play at school. Although my speaking voice was distinctly "middle-class Surrey", I was accomplished at fitting in with all kinds of people and found it easy to imitate accents. This proved to be good practise for an aspiring actor.

Sad to say that as we mature, we tend to outgrow childhood friends, especially when interests change. So, it was inevitable that Frankie and I would gradually drift apart, just as with my boarding school friends, although I am still in touch with some of them.

Many years later I read Pattie's book. Although I am not a sentimental, weepy person, I was reduced to tears when I realised how badly she had been treated by the egotistical men she had married and been left with little money after her beauty had faded. Having been the inspiration for three classic pop songs dedicated to her, one would have thought that Eric Clapton or George Harrison might have shared some of their huge royalty cheques with her.

I had lunch at her house not long ago. It was a nice cottage in Surrey but certainly not the mansion you would imagine a legendary "rock chick" to be living in. She appeared to have lived her youth in a world full of egos, drugs, and no real moral values, and although she seemed quite happy with her life, there was a sadness about her that made me think that being the wife of two eminent rock stars wasn't as great as one would think. You know how people put a montage of photographs on their toilet walls? Well, you can imagine the amazing photos Pattie has on her walls, with the "Fab Four" and the rest of the pop idols at the time cavorting about on Caribbean beaches and smoking joints at festivals. I wished I'd had a smart phone so I could have recorded them all.

What an amazing change it was to go from a convent school to a stage school, where the rules were minimal and the only reason for expulsion would be lack of talent or for committing a serious offence like stealing.

One particularly quiet, rather reserved female student, not known for being rebellious, secretly disappeared after stealing all sorts of things: purses, clothes, shoes. She must have been a kleptomaniac. She finally got caught after stealing Anne Rogers' shoes, a small size three, but the same size as hers, but not before she had made off with a favourite dress my mother had made for me and which I had worn in a Wall's ice cream commercial.

The second person to leave under a cloud was a lovely, talented, funny boy, Raymond Woodbine, who thought it would be a good idea to put a used Durex condom he had found outside (they were frequently seen outside in the gutters at that time) into the English teacher's coffee. Oh, the tense atmosphere as we waited to see her lift the cup to her lips, only for Sandra Bryant to shout out at the very last minute, "Don't drink that, Miss!" This misdemeanour could not go unpunished, so, sadly we never saw Raymond again.

We had some very interesting teachers at Conti's. Irskine Jones was a camp American jazz dance teacher. A great deal of hip movement went into his choreography. "Step, kick! Step, kick! Bump to the left and bump to the right and a hip roll," he would demand. Mrs Helen Volkes, the singing teacher, was a beautiful silver-pink-haired lady in a smart grey suit, with red lipstick and nails and a permanent lit cigarette clenched in her mouth while she banged away at the piano and gave effusive praise for our efforts. I ended up having extra singing lessons with her, as she thought I had potential for musical theatre. I believe I did, but in those days we didn't have radio mics, so you had to have a very big voice to compete onstage. At most auditions I attended I was up against Millicent Martin, who had a huge voice, so there was very little chance of me filling the London Palladium. My first professional theatre job was playing the part of Sailor Doll in *Noddy in Toyland* at the Victoria Palace in London. My friend, Colin Spaull, played the part of Noddy. We still see each other today, as we play golf with the Vaudeville Golfing Society. It was such an amazing experience to be on a West End theatre stage, albeit just for a Christmas show.

Sometimes, my father would pick me up from school, as he worked round the corner in Charing Cross Road. He would call me over to his Armstrong Siddeley Sapphire and give me instructions for the tobacconist next door. "Sixty untipped Player's for your mother, and sixty Senior Service for me. Ten Rothmans for yourself?" We would travel home, puffing away on our ciggies, me lying on the back seat, ashtrays in all the cars back then, and it seemed everybody smoked. We had silver cigarette boxes for visitors, and my dad had a gold cigarette case that he bought off a friend who needed the money.

At this time, I became even more fascinated with boys, despite the fact I had a brother. I had spent quite a time at single-sex schools without getting to know the opposite sex and suddenly discovered how really very nice boys are: they are not as cunning and manipulative as girls. I laughed at their jokes and hung out with them, which caused people to think I was an outrageous flirt. The truth was, I was quite innocent and had no idea about the kind of reaction I caused. Later, I realised that but still to this day get on equally well with men and women.

We had an hour's break at lunchtime and that's when we discovered the 2i's Coffee Bar in Old Compton Street, Soho, where you could play all the latest tunes on the jukebox.

The young people who came into this coffee bar were very much into music. There were even lunchtime jiving sessions with a sixpence entrance fee. I have never had a problem going out alone and often visited places by myself. I got to know some of the regulars at the 2i's. One was a redheaded boy called Ian Samwell, who was very sweet and bought me cappuccinos and told me he was a songwriter. I tended to take such information with a pinch of salt, as almost everybody who came into this coffee bar claimed they were something or other in the music business.

One day, Ian came in and told me he had written a song about me and called it "High Class Baby". He said he had written it for Cliff Richard. Would you believe him? I wasn't inclined to do so, as show business is full of people making false claims. He said it was going to be on the B-side of a record. I never bought it but wish I had. Later, my-son-in law Martin found on Wikipedia a quote "'High Class Baby' was written for actress Julie Cracknell (married name), mother of singer Sarah Cracknell, who had spurned his advances. After its release it was banned by the BBC for mentioning the Cadillac car, a breach of advertising regulations." No wonder I never heard it on the radio; you can hear it on YouTtube. Also at that time, I met a singer called Vince Taylor. I saw him downstairs in the coffee bar, singing with a band. We started seeing each other and he probably lasted the longest period I ever went out with anyone; the relationship continued for a whole month!

My parents bought a new house in Ewell, Surrey. It was a beautiful Georgian building, large with eight bedrooms, and an enormous living room with a sprung floor which acted as a ballroom at times. My sister, Tina, was having and a birthday party and I asked Vince if he and his band would come and play. Tina picked them up from the 2i's in her car and drove them down to the house. This turned out to be a disappointment, as the band only knew three songs, which they played repeatedly until we put the record player on. Vince went on to become a pop icon in France and Switzerland but got into drugs and died quite young from an overdose. Sadly, this was something that I later experienced with other close friends. I didn't know anything about drugs at age thirteen and I very rarely drank alcohol. Gin and tonics were for parents and other grownups, not for our coffee bar culture.

The school also ran a theatrical agency and, courtesy of the agency, we were all expected to go for auditions as children, which were very exciting. Getting a part in a film or on television was what we all wanted. I was called to the office one day and given some pages of a film script called *The Lord of The Flies*. This adaptation of the book had a girl playing the spiteful, mean role and a few of us were to audition for Richard Brooks, the director. Eventually, there was a shortlist, and I was asked to go to the Wyndham's Theatre to audition again to finalise the casting, and I believe the audition was being filmed. Opportunities like this were quite frequent and we didn't ever raise our hopes until we got the role. You get used to rejection, as it is all part of the job.

I had been invited to go and see *West Side Story* one evening after school, so I decided to have my hair done and skipped a class to go to Robert Fielding Hairdressers in Regent Street, where a friend from home was a junior assistant. Alan Carmel, a Conti's student who was a close friend, knew where I was. All hell broke loose as Richard Brooks arrived at the office, asked to see me, and I was missing. Alan offered to get me. He arrived in a taxi, kept it waiting outside, dashed in, took out all my rollers and pushed me into the taxi. By the time we arrived back at Conti's, I was mortified. I had wet hair hanging down over my shoulders and was almost in tears as I was summoned to the office. The film at that time never got made. This often happens through a lack of funding, but the whole incident was a lesson to me not to bunk off school.

That summer my mother and father thought it would be a good idea for my sister Margaret and I to go on holiday together to Rimini, on the Italian Riviera. I mentioned earlier how liberal our parents were, but I'm not sure this time they had thought it through. Margaret was seventeen, and I was fourteen. We set off by train, that went all the way through northern Europe over the border into Italy, where we changed in Milan.

The first morning we decided to head for the beach in front of our hotel, where we were staying full board. A hot and sunny glorious sandy beach and sparkling Adriatic Sea – how lovely to have left grey, rainy England. We lay our towels on the beach and lay down to sunbathe. Out of the blue came swarms of tanned, handsome young men who surrounded us. Margaret whispered to me, "Tell them we are Polish if they ask." The attention was too much for me and I wandered off to lay on a beached pedalo to sunbathe and read my book. I watched as Margaret glided into the sea with her blond pre-Raphaelite hair and figure-hugging bathing suit and all the boys following her like adoring puppy dogs. I suppose in those early days after the war it was unusual to see fair-haired girls amongst all the dark-eyed exotic signorinas.

That night after dinner Margaret had arranged to meet two of the boys, Felice and Mario, at our hotel. They were taking us to a roof-top lounge with music and dancing, a beautiful place underneath the stars with people laughing and dancing to a live band and a handsome singer in a white suit. I wore a summer dress with my hair in a ponytail, hoping to look older than I was.

The waiter came to take our order for drinks. Just then, I saw a tray with another waiter go by with glittering emerald-green cocktails. "I would like one of those, please," I said, thinking it would be a soft drink like lime juice. It turned out to be Crème De Menthe Frappe, a very strong alcoholic liqueur.

Mario asked me where in Poland I came from. I replied, "Very near to the capital." Then I changed the subject. I remember drinking the delicious green cocktail, but after that I don't remember anything else until I found myself back in my hotel bed with a doctor, Margaret, and a waiter to interpret looking at me. I felt terrible, a very bad headache and sickness. The waiter had a packet in his hand and told me that the doctor thought I had sunstroke and I would have to stay in a cool, dark room until I felt better, and that I must take this medicine. He showed me a large torpedo pill and instructed me to insert it up the back, not the front, three times daily. I was amazed and only slightly relieved to not have to swallow such a gigantic pill. I managed to ruin the first attempt, as it did a U-turn and fell out down the toilet.

We whiled away the rest of the holidays chatting to our new friends and going for rides on their Vespas – every young Italian seemed to have one. Leaving hot, sunny Italy snaking over the Alps and the weather cooling down, I finally felt my sunstroke headache was gone. "Why did we have to be Polish?" I asked Margaret.

"Because English girls are easy," she replied.

TEENAGE WORKING YEARS

Travelling to London on the train from Ewell East to Victoria during the rush hour was fine, but in the 1950s and early 1960s the trains had small separate carriages. So, during the day, if you were going for an audition or meeting, you would sometimes encounter a flasher. For those of you who don't know what that means, a flasher is a man of any age who likes to display his genitals in public, especially to young girls. This often happened to me, as I liked to be alone on the train so I could practise singing out loud if I was auditioning for a musical or recite aloud scripts I might be learning.

As this was not always a good idea, I would bring a magazine and, if anyone was fumbling around the trouser area, I would bury myself behind the pages. One day I encountered one of these flashers on my way home. I got off the train at Ewell and came face to face with a guard. I said to him, "There is a man in that carriage doing something very rude and nasty."

The guard replied, "Well, dear, we throw them all out at Epsom!"

On one occasion, I was on the train travelling to London and a very handsome teenage boy came on board. He started to ask me some directions from Victoria to central London. By this time, I could have been a successful taxi driver having done the knowledge, as I knew just about every street in the West End of London. He was very polite and told me he was on a visit with his uncle to see the sights and was staying at the Dorchester hotel. I was fortunate to have been to this famous landmark hotel on many occasions, as the Foyle's Literary Luncheons were held in the ballroom. He introduced himself as Ahmet and asked me if I would like to come for dinner one night. I was a little hesitant, as I didn't know what my parents would think of me travelling back home at night from London. He then said that he would come and collect me in a chauffeur-driven limousine and make sure I got back in time. My mother was visiting a friend in Japan at the time, so I told my father and said I would be home by eleven. He didn't really respond very clearly, so when Ahmet rang me to make the arrangements, I was quite excited about that night at the Dorchester.

The car arrived in our drive at six p.m. and off we went to the hotel. On the way, he told me that I would be meeting some very important people from Saudi Arabia. I was quite impressed when he also mentioned that they were members of the Saudi Royal Family.

I had dressed in a cream silk dress with a beaded top and tied my hair back in a ponytail. At dinner, I sat next to Ahmet and one of the other men who was with the group. We chatted away and I was really delighted to have met such a charming and handsome boy, particularly as there was never any hint of racism in our family.

In the meantime, my father was reading a piece in the *Evening Standard* about the prince staying at the Dorchester and entertaining young girls. He immediately put two and two together and flew into a panic as thoughts of the white trade slave trade and trafficking and prostitution went through his mind. We were just coming to the end of the meal when the prince suggested we all go to the Edmundo Ross nightclub. I declined and made excuses about having to be home early, but he was adamant that I should go and made out that it would be very disrespectful if I didn't. To save further embarrassment, I went along and sat next to Ahmet, as I felt he was my only ally.

Then some other older ladies joined the table and made the most of the hospitality and expensive champagne. The prince asked me to dance with him, which I did, and put on a bit of a show so that he would think I was enjoying myself. He then came to sit next to me. I told him about my grandfather and the shop and how famous my grandfather was, and how I had visited the Dorchester hotel many times. Then he got up to go to talk to one of his men, and I told Ahmet that I had to leave, as if I was not home by eleven, my father, who was very strict, would call the police. Ahmet spoke to the prince, who summoned a waiter to make a phone call, and within minutes a car was outside waiting to take me home. Ahmet came with me to see that I got home safely.

All hell broke loose when we drove into the drive. Ahmet was physically dragged out of the car and given a smack then told that if he ever dared call me again, my father would have him arrested. Ahmet left hurriedly in the car, and I never heard from him again. I was very cross with my father, as I felt humiliated by him in front of Ahmet. I now realise why he was as anxious and concerned as he was at the time. Maybe I have a guardian angel watching over me or maybe it was that growing up in Soho, I had learned to be streetwise.

A new girl came to Conti's, Elizabeth Bowyer. She was great fun and very talented. We became good friends and are still in touch today. She joined me at the 2i's, and we have many happy memories of our emerging teenage years, growing up in Surrey with an easy route to the West End of London. We would often stay up after school to visit the coffee bars, especially the 2i's and the Heaven and Hell, which was on the barred school list. One day we decided to stay after school, as we had been invited for a drink by the singer Terry Dene at a flat in Soho which was owned by his manager, Larry Parnes. We climbed up some rickety stairs to a flat that was highly decorated with a gold-padded bar front with many bottles behind it. Larry was very flamboyant and welcoming. "Right, girls, what can I get you to drink?"

"Well, um, not sure ..." We didn't wish to appear too young and inexperienced (which, of course, we were).

"How about a gin and orange?" said Larry. A gin and orange sounded harmless, so that's what we had. Gin in a glass with a small amount of concentrated orange juice tasted very sickly and most definitely alcoholic. What I remember after two of those was making my way to the Greenline bus stop in Regent Street, getting on the bus and gluing myself to the window so I wouldn't miss my stop. I felt dizzy and nauseous and so wretched that when I finally left at my home bus stop, I vomited in the gutter. Suddenly, I felt someone take my arm and help me across the road. This kind person took me all the way to my front gate then disappeared. I had no idea who it was but was so grateful to be home.

Sobering up, I had to face the parents, of course. I let myself in, called out, "I'm home," ran upstairs, threw myself on the bed and slept until morning, determined never to drink gin again. Ever. I kept to that pledge until recently when I discovered the different flavoured gins with tonics.

My father still had contacts in show business and arranged for Liz and me to get jobs as chorus girls in the pantomime *Cinderella* in Kidderminster. Panto is probably one of the most hilarious jobs you can get in theatre. It is fun and it pays well, as there are usually two shows a day. Kidderminster was a centre known for carpet manufacturing and woollen products. It was by no means the West End of London with theatres on every corner, but at age fifteen it was a start and something to add to our performance experience. Our parents took us to where the pair of us had booked digs in a B&B, a short bus ride away from the theatre, It was a cold and miserable place run by a very mean old lady. We shared a small double bed in a freezing attic room, the breakfast was one rasher of bacon and one tinned tomato, and we were only allowed one bath a week.

Fortunately, there was a very lively pub next door to the theatre which had accommodation, and we moved in as soon as we could to a large upstairs room with twin beds, next door to two nice young lads in the show who were playing the Broker's Men. Their manager, Guy Robinson, had put them in panto to learn some stagecraft. The boys were musicians in the Johnny Kidd and the Pirates rock band. One was called Art Caddy, guitarist, and the other was Brian Gregg. We were rehearsing hard and not eating sensibly and eventually came down with colds and cold sores.

After the panto ended, Liz and I returned to school. Having taken the obligatory exams, we no longer had to study any academic subjects, which was a relief. Now we only needed to attend vocational classes. This enabled us to go for jobs in the business, and we regularly scanned the pages in *The Stage* newspaper, looking for work and auditions. I spotted one for dancers and hostesses at the Nell Gwynne Club in Soho. Well, we were trained now so why not, we thought. A group of us turned up at the club ready to audition, our practise clothes in our bags, to be met by a large man who was probably a bouncer. "Yes, girls. What can I do for you?" he asked. We explained we had come for the audition for dancing hostesses. We hadn't a clue what a hostess was, but it sounded quite respectable. After all, airline hostesses were usually very posh. We added that we were students at the Italia Conti stage school, which we thought would be suitable. "Sorry, loves. You are far too young for this place, so you better run along now." Going to school in Soho was an education, aside from the singing, acting, and dancing.

Art and the bass player, Brian, introduced Liz and me to Guy Robinson, their manager. Guy suggested that Liz and I form a sister act doing Everly Brothers covers! He agreed to give us tuition in his office in Shaftesbury Avenue, so we bought black pleated skirts and black tops and practised the harmonies. This was my first encounter with a dirty old man. He would ask Liz to go and get some coffees from the café downstairs then push me up against the wall and try it on with me. When he learned I wasn't giving in, he would do the same with Liz and I would get the coffee, knowing full well what she was in for. Today, he would have been prosecuted and maybe jailed for the sexual assault of under-sixteens, but in those days no one said anything. As a young girl or young woman, you just put up with it. How times have changed, especially with the "Me Too" revelations and scandals. Guy did appear to have an interest in our careers, though, so we carried on. After a while, we got bored with the meetings and all this fumbling and decided not to turn up any more. Then suddenly, he phoned and told us the good news. He had got us a nightclub job singing in South Africa, to which our parents said, "Absolutely no way!" Later, I learned he wrote a song, "Please Don't Touch Me". Shame he didn't apply it to his own behaviour.

Liz was beautiful, tall, and slender and met a modelling agent called Pat Larthe. She suggested that maybe I could get some modelling work too, so I went to his office and had an interview. Obviously, modelling was not what I wanted as a career, but it was a good way of getting some decent photos of yourself and earning some money.

My first job was at the Ideal Home Exhibition, modelling teenage underwear for the Triumph brand. It was great fun, but on the first day I noticed that they had spelled my name incorrectly. It was written as "July". The compere, an elegant middle-aged lady, introduced me, "And here we have July in a mint-green bra and matching panties and suspender belt." It sounded funny, so I giggled a lot. We were then asked to do a tour of Marshall and Snelgrove stores for Triumph and made quite a lot of money along the way. But catwalk modelling was hardly a step in the right direction. Soon after, I shot a lot of photo strip comics, pictures for *Jacky* and *Roxy*, the teenage magazines that came along behind comics. If you were around at that time, you would have seen the sort of scenario: girl meets boy, then boy dumps girl for best friend, then boy realises first girl was nicer and it all ends happily. These comics were aimed at twelve- to sixteen-year-olds and had "problem pages" and pop star interviews and lots of advertisements for make-up, hair, and Stephanie Bowman slimming garments. These were plastic knee-length pants to sweat off excess fat from your thighs and backside. The garments appeared to work until you had a drink of water, and then the weight went back on again.

One day, Pat Larthe asked me to come in for a casting session for a film producer called Val Guest; now that seemed more like it! Val was an American movie director/producer married to the lovely Yolande Donlan. After my interview was over, I was walking down Bond Street to get the tube to Victoria when this long, sleek American Oldsmobile car pulled up beside me. I had no idea who it was and turned my head away. "Hi, Julie, it's me, Val. Do you want a lift?"

"Oh, sorry. I didn't recognise you," I stammered.

"Do you want a lift? Where are you heading?" he asked. I stopped and thought about what mothers always tell us but felt somehow this would be all right. You became very streetwise growing up in Soho.

After a moment I replied, "Well, I'm going to Victoria Station to get the train home."

"I'll take you there," he said. "Get in." So, I did. He was very friendly and said he would like to cast me in his next film, *The Day the Earth Caught Fire*, a sci-fi film.

Shepperton Studios, *The Day the Earth Caught Fire*

That was the beginning of a very long friendship. Val was a great person, off whom I could bounce ideas. He called me his protégé and he suggested that I should perhaps try comedy. He came down to visit me and my parents (Dad was not impressed and thought the worst!). I played two small roles for him, which certainly helped me to get my foot on the ladder. He also paid for a well-known stills photographer, Cornel Lucas, to do a photo shoot with me and also introduced me to Bill Watts' theatrical agent, who took me on his as a client.

I was leaving behind my school days and now becoming what I always wanted, "a working actress", appearing in films and television and very rarely out of work. In the early days of soaps and television dramas, there were some memorable moments. One such moment was in *Emergency Ward 10*, where I played the girlfriend of a boy who had an accident and ended up in hospital. In every episode in which I appeared, I had to say practically the same lines of dialogue, which went something like this: "Are you feeling okay? Can I get you anything?" This is classic "hospital dialogue". In the last episode, I completely forgot which episode I was in, so instead of speaking, I started to plump up the boyfriend's pillows and tidy his bed. This was live television in front of seven million people. The stage manager knew immediately what to do when someone dries (forgets their lines), and she pressed the idiot button. The effect is to cut out the sound and she gave me my lines. I think I saw stars in that moment I was in such shock. My parents were watching the episode and didn't notice a thing, however.

Another moment of terror in the middle of a scene occurred when I was playing a young girl of fourteen in a hospital scene again and being broadcast live, but this time I was the victim of an attack and being questioned by the police. In each scene, you have one or two cameras pointing at you and a sound man with a long microphone standing on top of a moving platform and called a boom operator. I was just about to answer a question when the boom operator fell off the stand and onto my bed. I, of course, sat up and bandages went flying, and he was seen clearly in the shot with his headphones on. There was a simple action the BBC did when something went wrong and that was to film a card saying something like, "This programme will resume as soon as possible". We then went back to the start of the scene. Fortunately for everyone, especially actors, you now rehearse and shoot just as you do with feature films, so you can make as many mistakes as you like. You just do "take" after "take" until you get it right. I was becoming quite well known in television, particularly after having played an apprentice dressmaker in *The Rag Trade,* a BBC series with Sheila Hancock and Miriam Karlin.

Jerry Mill was the studio floor manager and such a kind and thoughtful man. I got to work with him a lot later in the BBC series *Crown Court* and other BBC shows. He went on to become a director at ATV. David Croft was also a great help in my career. Once you got a role in a BBC series or film, if you didn't fall over the furniture and you knew your lines, you would be in the casting directors' lists for small parts in all sorts of regular series such as *Z Cars* and *Dixon of Dock Green*. Something I really enjoyed doing was *The Mike and Bernie Winters Show*, which was light entertainment with sketches, music (songs) and comedy. Lionel Blair was the lead dancer and choreographer on these shows, and we played to a live TV audience with a half-hour warm-up before the show was televised.

In the first sketch of one of these shows, I was in a comedic parody of *The Beverly Hillbillies*, an American TV sitcom about a family who discover oil on their land, become very rich and move to Hollywood. I was playing the part of an accountant dressed in a very boring grey suit and with a grey wig and glasses. Lionel advised me to put on something glamorous to wear for the warm-up so the audience would not recognise me. He was right, of course, as this kind of entertainment was all about your personality and likeability from the audience point of view. I had forgotten about so many of those small TV and film roles, but they pop up from time to time on UK Gold and I can barely remember playing the characters. Sometimes, it's easier to Google myself to find out if there is some good play I'd forgotten about! I know I could find every bit of information on my career online, as nowadays your whole life is there, recorded somewhere on the World Wide Web.

Suffice to say I was making a very good living. One very memorable show I did was *The Avengers*. In this episode, I played the role of a fairground belly dancer, Rosie, who was linked to some dangerous gangsters that were being pursued by secret agent John Steed, played by Patrick Macnee. Poor Patrick, I had to hit him over the head with a fake plaster urn! Then began an unlikely friendship-romance once again with a huge difference in age. Yet again, I had to cope with a furious father and his negative reaction. However, I had a besotted mother, and Patrick played up to her in his characteristic gentlemanly way.

I can remember the many nights out at places like The Ivy, Caprice, and a wonderful Italian restaurant in Soho, Mario and Franco's, where I first tasted zabaglione, a delicious desert. I wanted to know how to make it, and Patrick called the chef, who gave me a demonstration in the kitchen: egg yolks, sugar and marsala wine, beaten until the mixture becomes an airy, light pale glass of froth. Irresistible! Patrick was a lot of fun. God only knows what his contemporaries, Ian Hendry, and his girlfriend, Janet Munro, thought of me. They must have thought it was very odd, a sophisticated man of his years taking out a sixteen-year-old girl. One night I nearly got Patrick shot. Before I met him, I had been dating a very nice, suitable, polite and well-educated boy called Tommy Wertheim, whom I met in a club called La Poubelle (French for dustbin), whose father had escaped from the Nazis in Germany during the war and who became a very successful button manufacturer. I had enjoyed my relationship with Tommy but being so young I did not want to be tied down.

Tommy soon realised I must have been seeing someone else, as I became unavailable too often. My mother had always advised a gradual break-up, as it was less painful. One night, unbeknown to me, Tommy was lying in wait in the unmade road outside our house. I spotted his little yellow Ford Anglia parked behind some bushes and realised there was going to be a scene.

Tommy got out of his car, very upset, and we saw he was carrying his father's wartime revolver. I told Patrick to drive away slowly and leave me to deal with Tommy.

With my knees knocking and heart pounding, I pleaded with Tommy to put the gun away. He did. We cried in each other's arms, knowing this was the end of our teenage relationship.

Many years later, I happened to be at my cousin Wendy's wedding reception at the Kensington Palace Hotel when I saw on a noticeboard that there was another wedding in another function room. I peeped in and it was Tommy's wedding. I caught site of his brother, Anthony, and we smiled at each other.

Patrick and I split up when I went to Bath to play the Fairy Queen in *Goldilocks and the Three Bears*. He came to see me in the panto, and we stayed at a hotel near the theatre. By then, both of us realised there was nothing left between us but a friendship.

My agents were Bill and Cherry Watts, who represented many glamorous film stars such as Joan Collins and Shirley Ann Field, a charming and caring couple who took me under their wing. I would call every day to see what work I had coming up. In retrospect, this was a good thing to do, as I was very rarely out of work. One day I went out very early and missed their call, so they called my parents to see if I was unwell. I am not sure if agents today make daily calls to their clients expressing interest and concern.

"ME TOO" DILEMMA

At this point in my career, I must mention "Me Too" episodes. Should any new actor read this, let it be a lesson to you, although following the Harvey Weinstein court case, I would imagine that anyone in a position of power in the business would be extremely cautious about the way in which they deal with aspiring actors. The first encounter was with a famous Hollywood film producer called Frank G Rosenberg. I got a call from Bill Watts to say he would like me to come for an audition at the Dorchester. I was sent up to Frank's suite and knocked on the door. It was opened by an aging, balding, overweight man in a silk dressing gown with clearly nothing on beneath it. I immediately apologised for being early, assuming he had just come out of the shower. "Please, do come in," he said as he beckoned me to sit on the sofa. I sat down and he offered me a drink. I declined the offer and he started to tell me about the part that he wanted me to read for. "The film's about young girls hitch-hiking around Europe in the summer break." I asked if I could see the script, but he told me that currently it was just a storyline, and the script was being written at that moment.

I was beginning to feel uncomfortable but decided to carry on as if it were perfectly normal to be sitting next to a man who was naked under a dressing gown. He then asked me to stand up. I was wearing a smart little navy-blue dress with a full skirt and petticoats. He asked if I could please take off the dress, as he needed to see my figure because the girl I was to play would be in shorts, T-shirts and a bikini. I dutifully did this and stood there in my underwear while he scrutinised my figure. I made a move to put my dress back on, but he told me not to do so, as we were going to do a bit of improvisation together. "So, we are lovers and we have had a row and you want to make it up to me."

Right, I thought, this is all going too far, so I jumped up and said, while climbing into my clothes, "Oh! Is that the time? I'm so sorry, but I'll have to leave, as my mother will be waiting for me at the station and I'll miss my train. She worries, as I am only fifteen." He immediately jumped up and fumbled in his wallet, pulled out a ten-shilling note and told me to get a taxi.

I told Bill about the meeting, and he didn't seem to be at all surprised. I expect there was a lot of that going on in those days. Funnily enough, though, I got a handwritten Christmas card from Frank and his wife for the next ten years!

Here is another lesson for any aspiring young actors reading my story. I was asked to read for a new film being made at Pinewood Studios. The producer was an American called Marty Pol. He could have been a casting director, as I couldn't find him on IMDB. The meeting was to be held in another London hotel suite, in Sloane Square. He had a script that was a comedy and suggested we read it together. We laughed a lot, and he was quite young and attractive, so when he asked me if I would have dinner with him, I did. We ended back upstairs in the hotel with a bottle of wine. One thing led to another, and we ended up in bed. Three weeks later, the phone rang. My father answered it and said, "There's a Yank on the phone for you, Julie."

I answered it and the voice on the other end said, "Hi, Julie. This is Mike here. I'm a friend of Marty's and I'm in London for a few days and wondered if you would like to come out with me. Marty said you like a good time." Well, I was mortified! He made me feel like a call girl.

There were lots of other incidents too, where there was a suggestion that I might have a better chance of getting the job if I was a nice, friendly girl, but I never fell into that trap again.

Another memorable incident was probably the worst, with the most disgusting lowlife creature called Allen Klein, who was briefly associated with the Beatles and the Rolling Stones. Once again, I was asked to go to the Dorchester hotel. This is where many Americans liked to stay and was becoming quite notorious in my head. I was asked to read for the film *Mrs Brown, You've*

Got a Lovely Daughter. I wasn't keen, as it was another light pop film, this time starring Peter Noone from the band Herman's Hermits. This was hardly going to be in the same league as a film with the Beatles or Gerry and the Pacemakers, and I was not interested in playing another pop star's girlfriend. Allen Klein was with Bobby Vinton, an American pop singer who had a hit with a song called *She Wore Blue Velvet*. There were four of us waiting in an anteroom. One by one, each of us was invited into the main room to have a chat and read a couple of lines from the script. I was asked to stay behind, as was another pretty, dark-haired actress. After the other two girls had left, Allen came out and offered us a drink and we sat chatting for a while. Then Allen asked me to go back into his room where he had a desk and blatantly said that if I gave him a blow job, the role was mine. I was appalled and left the room. He then asked the other girl to go in. I grabbed my bag, but Bobby tried to block my exit, asking why I didn't stay and have another drink. I couldn't get out of there fast enough and really hope this kind of behaviour is a thing of the past.

THE FILM THAT CHANGED MY LIFE

Bill Watts called to ask me if I would like to go to Yugoslavia to join an American film company for a movie called *The Long Ships*. The casting director was looking for English-speaking actresses to go out and play any small speaking parts that came up. The casting director had seen me in *The Plane Makers*, a television series starring Patrick Widmark, and approached my agent to see if I was available. It was a great opportunity to meet top-ranking directors and people in the international film industry. Three of us went out to Yugoslavia: Pamela Greer, Talitha Pol, and me.

Viking Wenches, *The Long Ships*

Our first location was in Lim Bay, now in Croatia, with a hotel overlooking a valley which is rather like a fjord. Most of the filming here was of the ships coming in and out of the valley and Vikings landing on the quay. We were not needed for this part of filming but were there to be fitted with costumes and wigs for the next location. Being marooned as we were in the middle of nowhere, we made our own entertainment after work. This involved turning the dining room into a night club and dancing. I was the youngest person in the company, and actor Richard Widmark was quite worried about me. He came to my room to give me books, and the naughty stunt boys jumped into bed with me to watch his reaction. He didn't show any kind of surprise and just ignored them.

Film crews are like travelling circuses, full of exciting people all sharing the same interests. There is a great deal of drinking, partying, womanising, and of making as much money as possible and the bigging up of expenses. It doesn't matter where you are, film crews will manage to turn a room into a night club. We did this in Budva, Montenegro. Our hotel was awful by today's standards, but we didn't mind, as we were all having so much fun. Naturally, everyone wanted to have been a part of a timeless film that has artistic merit and a commercial success everyone remembers, but although this film is often on TV, it never made it into that category. There are quite a few continuity faults in the film, if you look carefully, but when you are only seventeen, you don't feel you to need to worry about the future, as you are living for the moment. Perhaps this is also what we should be doing as we get older. We had some very famous American actors in the film – Richard Widmark, Sidney Poitier, Russ Tamblyn, Rosanna Schiaffino (a buxom actress like Gina Lollobrigida) – and some well-known British actors – Edward Judd, Gordon Jackson, and the very funny actor, Lionel Jeffries, who played a eunuch. Most of the crew were British and one particular evening, I danced all night with the cute and cheeky Russ Tamblyn.

We finally moved to the Metropol Hotel in Belgrade, the capital of then Yugoslavia, now the capital of Serbia. In Belgrade's Avala Studios, all the interior shots were filmed. We travelled on the Trans-Siberian Express, which was like being in an Agatha Christie crime scene, with Eastern-European men smoking cigars and drinking vodka. I shared a cabin with a gay hairdresser. Travelling was quite an experience in a train with red velvet upholstery and polished wood. I think that train may still exist somewhere. It is probably employed as one of those advertised train holidays like the Orient Express experience.

The Metropol was the best hotel in Belgrade, and the city was so interesting, with its mix of old and new buildings. The country was ruled by a communist regime at that time and General Tito was in charge. We had to be careful how we behaved in public, as a third assistant said something out of place and was immediately deported back to England. The hotel was quite luxurious for the time and very busy. I had started to hang out with Russ and really enjoyed his company. I especially liked dancing with him. He was good fun, and it was nice to have a partner. It was a platonic relationship; well, almost!

While we were there, the producer, Irving Allen, arrived and he threw a cocktail party for the cast and crew. I got bored and went to bed early but was awakened in the middle of the night by a knock on the door to find two stunt men asking me if they could use my balcony. Dickie Graydon was known as the Gentleman Jim of the underworld. He had been a pupil at Stowe (the famous public school), but he was a secret cat burglar, who would climb up hotel walls and steal jewellery from wealthy American heiresses. On this night, they wanted to know who was spending the night with the producer. It happened to be Talitha. I was saddened by this, for why would an attractive girl like that feel she needed to sleep with the producer when she was already working on a major film? I spoke to her the next day. She told me that as a child, she had lived in complete poverty (she and her mother were held in a Japanese prisoner-of-war camp), and she always worried she would end up in poverty. Peter Sarstedt wrote a song, "Where Do You Go To My Lovely", and it could have been written for her. She later married one of the richest men in the world, John Paul Getty, but sadly died of a drug overdose.

Money doesn't always bring happiness, as we know.

In our first scenes, we were to be in a bacchanalian Viking party, celebrating the king's birthday. We were dressed as serving wenches, in specially designed sackcloth dresses, with fake tans and blond wigs and had to fly around filling up pottery mugs with mead. I had my second urn-bashing scene where I had to hit stuntman Alf Joint on the head with another urn.

photo of the urn bashing

They were roasting an ox on the set, but by the end of that scene, the carcass was infested with rats. For those who don't know about filming, you usually manage to shoot between two to three minutes a day, and that carcass was on set for weeks. One day I was called to the set to play the small part of a concubine to the Viking king, played by actor Oscar Homolka. He was a Hungarian character actor in his sixties. In the scene, I was to be in bed with him. Oh dear. My nerves were shot to pieces, for he was old enough to be my grandfather.

This is where I first met Derek Cracknell. He was the second assistant director. The first assistant director (AD) was Bluey

Hill, a legendary filmmaker with a reputation for being tough and a hard-drinking hell raiser. One night, his driver dropped him off at the hotel he had been drinking at with the Yugoslavian crew. He spent the entire night in the lift, going up and down with the guests, until his driver picked him up in the morning and drove him to work. Another night, we were sitting in the dining room and a flaming bedspread flew past the window. Bluey had fallen asleep with a lit cigarette in his hand, and set his bed on fire. I am surprised he never got the sack, but he certainly knew his job.

Derek was very handsome, in a dark, brooding way, with a lovely smile. I was nervous about the scene and had just lit up a cigarette while the make-up artist was busy tanning my body when I heard a voice say, "Little girl, we do not smoke on a film set." Those were his first words to me, which made me feel small and foolish. I was determined to get my own back in time and certainly did later.

Derek Cracknell

After a couple of weeks, we had other cast members arrive to join the crew. These were beautiful and exotic girls who were cast to play Sidney Poitier's harem. We joined them in being fitted for harem costumes, designed by Paco Rabanne (no expense spared there). Paco designed the costumes around individual photographs of each of us and then drew pictures of us in the costume. I was small with small breasts, and my costume was beautiful shades of pink: flowing harem pants and a turban. I was also fitted with a long black glossy wig. However, there was no top, except for cerise-coloured metal nipple covers that I had to stick on with eyelash glue. You would never have known it was the same actress who played the Viking wench in sackcloth!

Harem Girls

58

Our now extended group of girls used to sit in the studio canteen, fully clothed and made up, ready for the sultan's harem scene and playing poker and hearts with our expenses money. Most of the girls would be drinking Slivovitz brandy and Turkish coffee. At the end of each day, we used to meet in the bar after dinner, as there was no television set in our rooms. So, we spent a lot of time socialising together. One night, Derek was standing at the bar with other crew members when he caught my eye and winked. Dawn Brooks, who was a feisty British actress living in Rome and who had arrived with the other girls, dared me to go and sit next to him and get him to ask me out. Never one not to take up a challenge, I boldly sashayed up and asked to buy him a drink. He did, of course, buy me a drink. I didn't drink alcohol in those days, just Coke, but decided to have a vodka and tonic to appear grown up. The alcohol went straight to my head, but I kept myself in check and arranged to go out for dinner with him the following night. I turned around to signal a thumbs up to my group then turned back to see those deep blue eyes and fell madly in love for the first time.

Luka, one of the crew members from the Yugoslavian studio, invited us to visit his mother in a farmhouse in the rural area a couple of hours outside Belgrade. Dawn had her boyfriend, Russell Rooks, who was visiting. We set off on a Friday night, crammed into Derek's Volkswagen Beetle, and headed off into unknown territory. After an hour, we stopped at a railway crossing with a closed barrier. It was getting dark and there were no lights or signals around, so we decided it must be a manually operated crossing.

Derek and Russell went to lift the barrier and managed to get it close to the top. Just then, an express train came rattling through and the barrier carried on up electronically. A few minutes later and we would all have perished.

The farmhouse was in a small hamlet surrounded by fields, Although the house was quite large, there were only two bedrooms. Luka's mother welcomed us at the door with the customary glass of Slivovitz and a bowl of soup. It was late and we decided to go to bed. All four of us were shown to a large bedroom with a sink and a huge double bed in which we were all expected to sleep. As you can imagine, there was a lot of giggling and decisions to be made regarding who was going to be in the middle and who on the edge.

I always rise early, so I slipped out of bed, leaving my bedfellows asleep, and went downstairs to find the toilet. Even by European standards, it was primitive. The toilet was a piece of antique Chippendale, more of an elaborate commode, with a stepladder and a circular lid on top which you removed to reveal the bowl. Where the contents went after that, who knows?

In the kitchen garden, the mother was playing with a lamb, which was jumping around in the garden. Little did I know that it would be served up for lunch.

Derek and I moved into a flat for the remaining weeks in the city. It was small but cosy and gave us time to spend time together and to get to know each other. Finally, we began to film the harem scenes in our beautifully elaborate costumes. We were given a tanning treatment and I had the long glossy black wig, which I loved. I finally had a few lines of dialogue, leaning over a palace balcony and sizing up the Viking stunt men. The palace was spectacular, with an elaborate hall and an ornamental pool. The final scene was of the Vikings invading the palace and supposedly raping the women in an orgy scene. As we were captive women, we were supposed to be willing to have fun with them. Dawn was asked to swing from a pillar on a chiffon rope into the pool. Unfortunately, the pool was lined with sharp tin. We watched with horror as the water slowly turned red. An ambulance was called, and Dawn ended up in hospital where they patched her up. The scars on her shins healed, but she was scarred for life. Fortunately, she was paid a huge sum of money from the film's insurance company and was able to go back to work in New York.

While I was filming, I got news that my beloved grandfather William had died of a stroke. I was devastated at not being able to get home for his funeral, but flights in those days were few and unreliable. Before leaving Belgrade, I discovered that Derek had kept a secret from me. A letter for Derek arrived at the flat we shared in Belgrade. Dawn suggested I steam it open just in case it was something important. It was, I discovered, a bombshell. Derek was already engaged to an airline stewardess called Shirley Shannon. I kept his secret and waited to find out about this from him directly. I stayed with the film and crew when they went to the beautiful island of Sveti Stefan in Montenegro.

It was another week before Derek and I were able to have a romantic dinner, having travelled five hundred miles in his battered VW to this beautiful island. That was when he admitted to me that she was coming out to join him on location. She was much older than me and he had known her for a few years. I was devastated to discover this and was left feeling gutted and used. I returned home with a broken heart. I was learning about life very fast. It was the beginning of June 1961, and I was just seventeen.

MENDING A BROKEN HEART WITH WORK

My agent sent me to Manchester Granada Television to do three episodes of *Coronation Street*. I was to be Jennifer Moss' friend in the episodes. I don't remember much about this, except that I stayed in the Midland Hotel and the whole cast of *Coronation Street* was warm and welcoming and Jennifer took me to all the clubs in Manchester. I spent quite a few weeks in Manchester, playing more parts in various other productions. When I came back to London, I got a sudden phone call from Derek, asking to see me again. I was reluctant to start up again after being so hurt, but I gave him an ultimatum and the weekend to tell her the truth; only then would I be prepared to meet him.

He rang me after the weekend and told me he was no longer engaged to Shirley and that she had learned of our affair from some crew members on the film. Poor Derek, he then had to meet my family, who grilled him relentlessly, but they all learned to love him later. My parents had decided to move to Burnham-on-Crouch in Essex to be close to my grandmother now that she was alone. As we were all either working or studying in London, we were not able to join them. My mother asked me and my brother Bill to find a flat in London and said she would help with the rent for a few months until we were on our feet. Bill and I found a nice two-bedroom mansion flat in Longridge Road in Earl's Court. My sister Tina was married, and my other sister, Margaret, was with her boyfriend Jack in North London.

I was spending most weekends with Derek in Richmond, as it was convenient for work, being so close to London and the studios. I was getting a lot of TV and film work at that time. My agent rarely considered theatre. Why would he when he was earning so much from the better-paid TV work? It was a pity though, as I really enjoyed working in theatre. It wasn't long before Bill moved out of the Earl's Court flat to be with Bente, his first wife, and I was spending most weekends with Derek in Twickenham.

HITTING THE BIG TIME

More like getting another rung up the ladder. Around this time, I auditioned for the film *Ferry Cross the Mersey*. It was the first leading role I had been up for, and I was quite excited and hopeful that I would get it. Brian Epstein and Michael Holden were the producers, and Jeremy Summers was the director. I had to jump through quite a few hoops to get the part, including several screen tests before meeting up with Gerry Marsden to make sure he approved of me too. The stars of the film were the pop group Gerry and the Pacemakers, who at the time were vying with the Beatles to take the pop world's crown. It never happened, but the group had many hit records, and Gerry had a long and successful career touring and recording until his sad death in 2021.

Also in the film, with a cameo role and song, was Cilla Black. I was fascinated both by her and by how her boyfriend, Bobby, was so attentive, even to the extent of carrying her comb and mirror. Cilla was exactly as we had always known her, down to earth, funny, and so very talented with an unforgettable voice. We had an enormous amount of promotion work to do on the film, including a press reception, and many TV appearances such as Ready Steady Go, a popular youth program on Friday nights.

I never imagined how frantic fans could be. Many times, we had to be smuggled out of back doors or had to make a run for the car, which would then be covered with teenage girls trying to get in. I was most unpopular as the love item in the film, and on a number of occasions, narrowly avoided being attacked. Most times, we had a group of security men with us who would bodily lift the girls off cars before we would speed off. Mary Quant, who was just beginning to be a recognised as a new designer, designed the clothes for the film, and Vidal

Sassoon cut my hair into a bob. The bob didn't last long, as the film's hairdresser had other ideas. There was no assistant director booked, so I suggested Derek, as he had recently been elevated to a first assistant.

PR photo for **Ferry Cross the Mersey**

Filming started in Twickenham Studios for all the interior shots. That was convenient for me, as it was ten minutes down the road from where Derek and I were living. It was Gerry's first time as an actor. He did well with learning all the lines, and how to hit your mark, and how not to look into the camera. He had a natural charm and a great sense of humour. I had a problem understanding the boys to begin with but soon got accustomed to the Liverpool dialect, occasionally mimicking the accent and having to be reminded that I was supposed to be posh. Having completed the interior shots we relocated to Liverpool, staying at the very grand Adelphi Hotel for the location shots. Having recently visited this hotel, I was sad to see it had gone into decline. All the once-beautiful Georgian features were crumbling. Like many other well-known period hotels, it had lost the splendour of its original period.

In one scene, I had to drive a Triumph Spitfire, but there was one snag: I didn't drive. The production manager found an army instructor to train me every day after filming. After ten days I took a driving test. I failed. However, the good old Liverpool police allowed me to drive while filming. Driving and acting at the same time is quite an art, especially when you have the whole camera crew perched on the back of a very small car and you are still uncertain about which is first gear and which is second gear! What were they thinking of, allowing a teenage girl without a driving licence to drive through the centre of Liverpool? In one shot I was to drive down a ramp towards the ferry and put the brakes on, but the weight of the car just kept propelling me forward. Fortunately, I managed to stop just before the River Mersey! We had a hound dog on the film, not for any real purpose, but I found out later he was on a daily rate and was earning more money than I was.

Nothing compares to the fees that are paid to the big box office stars today, but for a teenager in those days, I was paid a lot of money. I spent the money on clothes, shoes, etcetera. Well, who wouldn't? We had some wonderful locations in Liverpool. One scene was shot in the Cavern Club, where all the Liverpudlian musicians played during the 1960s. We then relocated to the Empire Theatre for the talent competition scenes. Jimmy Savile was the host in that scene. To be honest, I found him very creepy and stayed well clear of him. We had a break during the filming in Liverpool. It was a long Bank Holiday weekend, so Derek and I decided to go to North Wales for a seaside trip. We stayed first in Prestatyn then travelled over to Anglesey, which was beautiful and where we stayed in an old, rather charming hotel called the Treader Bay Hotel. We had a lovely romantic meal on the way then stopped off at a small jewellery shop to buy a wedding ring. It is hard to believe nowadays, but back then, it was frowned upon to share the same hotel room if you were unmarried, so we always checked in as Mr and Mrs Cracknell. We were all sad when the film ended and we went our separate ways.

I was offered a leading TV role in a Granada production called *Virginia*. Once again, I was off to Manchester to rehearse and record the show. The film was about a young girl who was a virgin and who had a slow decline into madness. It was rather strange, as I ended up pacing the streets clutching a teddy bear.

BIG CHANGE OF DIRECTION
AT TWENTY YEARS OLD

Shortly after my agent rang to tell me that United Artists wanted to put me under contract for further films. It felt incredible, for this was just the beginning of reaching my goal. I flew back from Manchester feeling very unwell. During the flight, I locked myself into the toilet to be sick, assuming I had eaten something and had food poisoning. It was arranged for me to have a medical examination. This is quite common, for if you are contracted to a company for any length of time, the film company needs insurance in place in the event you might be taken unwell, or have an accident, during filming. I remember the doctor asking me some personal questions about my periods. I couldn't remember when the last one was, Oh, my god! It suddenly dawned on me that I might be pregnant. The doctor did a blood test and told me he would be in contact when he had the results. He called a couple of days later to tell me that I was probably five weeks pregnant. That romantic night in Anglesey was to change my life forever. I was so shocked and so very scared I went to stay with Derek. He, and his best friend Al, told me it would be better to terminate it now in the early stages.

Al knew of a doctor who could perform the termination. I cried bitterly all night, as I did not want to abort a baby that Derek and I had produced together. Derek was adamant that we were not in the right place to have a baby and felt too that it would ruin my blossoming career. The next day I went back to my flat in London and decided to talk to my older sister, Tina. I told her about the dilemma, and she also felt I would very much regret terminating a baby. I was beginning to feel emotional about it all and decided that whatever decision I made would not include a continuing relationship with Derek. I knew how he was thinking, and in my mind at that time, it meant that he had no real deep feelings for me. Once again, he broke my heart, and I cried all night. I was devastated but cut all communication with him, as it only made me unhappy.

After a few days I was packing to go down to face my parents in Burnham to tell them the news when he turned up on the doorstep. He hugged me and told me that whatever I wanted to do, he would stand by me. I felt an enormous surge of relief knowing I did not have to face this alone, and together we travelled down to Burnham to face the music. My mother was instantly worried about what my grandmother and the neighbours would say. My father was livid, for in his eyes I had thrown away my career, a career that could have been his if his health had been better. I totally understood but argued that I could manage both things, motherhood and acting. In those days, unless you were an established star, the struggle of juggling motherhood with an acting career was not easy. However, both my parents liked Derek a lot, welcomed him into the family, and my mother immediately started planning for the wedding. She remained worried about my grandmother finding out about the pregnancy so invented a rushed excuse, saying that, as we both had forthcoming jobs, we needed to get married before I was due to go to Ireland to accompany Derek on location for the film *The Blue Max*. The wedding reception was at Beeleigh Abbey, catered by Harrods and attended by all the family friends and Cracknell family members. Aunty Chrissy gave me a bag full of cash, so I discreetly went the toilet, sat on it as if it were a throne and counted out every note. Pity I didn't have a picture of that.

This would never happen today, as I no longer really feel the need for formality and signed documents that try to guarantee you remain monogamous with someone, but I wanted to protect my parents from any scandal that my actions might cause. So, we all went ahead with the arrangements. By this time, Bill and I had given up the flat in Earl's Court and I had moved in with Derek and his best friend, Al Mitchell. We made an odd threesome but got on very well. Being pregnant made me feel maternal, and I was happy to shop and cook for the three of us and to keep the flat tidy.

Wedding group

I was suffering terrible morning sickness and didn't feel much like taking on any acting work, but I did do an episode of *Box Jury*. I bought some orange cotton fabric and made myself a dress that accentuated my growing bosom and minimised my expanding waistline. In any event, my bump was well hidden behind a desk. We also had the first press showing of *Ferry Cross the Mersey*, which Derek and I attended. My mother had arranged for me to stay with them in Burnham-on-Crouch for my confinement, as Derek was working away on location, and she wanted to keep an eye on me. My lovely daughter, Sarah, was born a week early on the 12th April 1965.

I was to give birth at the nursing home in Burnham-on-Crouch, but because of complications I was taken to St John's Hospital in Chelmsford. I had pre-eclampsia, and my blood pressure was sky high. Fortunately, I had already gone into labour, and everything turned out fine. Only the doctors were with me, and I felt very scared, Derek came all the way from London to sit with me for a while. Eventually, I sent him away, as he nearly fainted when the nurse fitted a drip into the back of my hand, and I thought the sight of me giving birth would tip him over the edge. In a way, I was glad for him not to be there to see all the gore and medical procedures that come with giving birth. Whilst it is very different today, in those days, husbands were not encouraged to be with their wives during labour and birthing. Back then, it was deemed to be primarily a female occasion, with midwives in attendance, and sometimes too, a doctor, like an episode of *Call The Midwife*.

The next morning, I was transferred to the little nursing home in Burnham-on-Crouch, which had been freshly painted to welcome its local celebrity! Every patient had their own bedroom and there was even a friendly dog that would pace up and down the corridor and visit the new mothers and check out the new-born babies. This would not be allowed today. It was also customary to stay in hospital for almost a week, to ensure that new mothers got plenty of rest in preparation for the sleepless nights they would suffer later.

How considerate and civilised that was, unlike today when patients get chucked out as soon as possible. At night, the baby would be removed if it was restless and given an extra bottle of milk by a nurse to calm it down.

Derek came to stay as soon as he could, and he and my father came to pick me up. Unlike me, Derek was a natural parent. As the oldest of five children, he knew exactly how to hold babies, change nappies, and give bottles. They arrived at the nursing home to pick me up on a bicycle! It was just a joke, as my dad had the car hidden around a corner, but they kept up the joke, much to the furious reaction of Matron, who refused to allow them anywhere near me and the baby. Sarah was a lovely baby, pink, blond and pretty.

Soon, we all fell into a routine. Derek would wake up early, bring Sarah into bed and we would have a little play. I would then feed her, he would go off to work, and I would do housewifely things and have a nice dinner on the table for his return. This may be a surprise to some of my friends, but I didn't drink alcohol in those days. It never occurred to me to get any wine or alcohol in the house, except if we had guests. We did have a drink when we went out for dinner, or to pub, but not every day as we do today.

Julie and Baby Sarah Picture Derek Cracknell

Derek went off to Ireland to continue filming *The Blue Max*, a First World War film about Count Von Klugermann (played by actor James Mason) and a young Lieutenant Bruno Stachel, a brash German fighter pilot (played by American actor George Peppard). The main filming was at Bray Studios in Ireland. Sarah was just three weeks old when we flew out to be with Derek, who had found a nice house for us in Bray, close to Dublin. The house was fine but not modern, with absolutely no useful kitchen tools at all. We had an Aga cooker but no fridge, washing machine or dishwasher, so I had my work cut out. We hired a lovely lady as a mother's help. Her name was Mrs Whelan and, having had nine children herself, there wasn't a thing she didn't know about babies. It was wonderful for me to have such an experienced lady around to show me the ropes.

I had my twenty-first birthday in Bray. Derek arranged a surprise party for me at the local hotel. He told me to go and buy a nice new dress and he would take me out to dinner. The party was at the Glenview Hotel in Wicklow, overlooking the rolling hills. Unbeknownst to me, the entire cast and crew were all waiting for me in a large ballroom. Ursula Andress and George Peppard were there, and what an amazing party it turned out to be. I could not believe how many people had bought me presents.

We had been in Ireland for a month when I got a call from my agent that director Lewis Gilbert wanted to see me for a part in a film called *Alfie*. So, I flew back to London for an interview. It was for the part of one of Alfie's girlfriends, who becomes pregnant. I was sad not to get the part. Lewis Gilbert told my agent that he didn't think I was "mumsy" enough, which was strange, as I was still breast-feeding Sarah.

We returned to England in July and had to rent a home, as the house we had bought was still being built. It was in Highgate, close to where my grandfather was buried in Highgate Cemetery. I used to pass by his grave on my way to the launderette with Sarah in the pram. Derek had started work on *2001: A Space Odyssey* with director Stanley Kubrick.

One day, I got a call from Derek to say they were looking for a baby to be the star child at the end of the film. A car came to take me and Sarah to the MGM studios in Elstree to have some film shot of her being held upside down by her ankles. She didn't seem to mind this, but she looked too cute and cuddly; the producers decided that they would have to mock up a foetus instead to represent the alien baby.

I had invested some money from *The Long Ships* into an investment bond and decided it would be good to use it as a deposit on a house near to Pinewood Studios. Derek was amazed, as he had only ever envisaged renting as he had always done. Twickenham was not within our financial range, so we searched further out in Berkshire and discovered the beautiful town of Windsor. Once we were settled in our new home, a small modern house in Edinburgh Gardens near Windsor Castle, it was time for me to go back to work. To enable me to attend auditions and meetings, we hired a Swiss au pair, Suzanne. Derek was offered *The Battle of Britain* and was based at Pinewood Studios and various airfields across the country. He always wanted us to join him wherever he was working. As Sarah was not yet at school, we visited him on many interesting and quite exotic locations. I even got to fly in a Spitfire.

I decided to do an acting course to get back some lost confidence, having been a stay-at-home mother. I had met an actor, Peter Layton, in an episode of *The Plane Makers*, and he had started acting classes in a hall in Ealing. He was an inspirational teacher and went on to open Drama Studio London, a successful school for postgraduate students. He specialised in nurturing individual talent and reminded me why I had become an actor in the first place.

Before long, I was offered the leading role in a television drama for ITV. It was directed by a woman called Valerie Hanson. She had been an actress in her younger days but had suffered an accident where she had disfigured her face so had become a director instead.

I played opposite a young unknown actor called Malcom McDowell, who later became a movie star in Hollywood. The play was complicated. I had to have a dual personality and speak with an upper-crust accent in one scene and then with a cockney accent in the next. It was difficult at first, as I didn't want to sound too false. I liked to be naturalistic when acting and felt the direction for me and for Malcom was far too dramatic for small-screen television. I felt my role needed to be slightly vulnerable, but Valerie was having none of it. There must be some empathy between a director and actor so they can work together on the characterisation of the role. I had heard about bullies in the business, but this was the first time I had become the victim. We had a very nice stage manager who warned me about Valerie's need to find a whipping boy, which, apparently, she did on every show. Sometimes, this resulted in grown men ending up in tears. Malcolm was very supportive and championed me against her, but one day, the sniping became too much, and I decided to walk out. It was the day before we did a full run, so I know it was not good for anyone, but both Derek and I felt that life was too short to put up with such nonsense. The writers had already been in and praised me for my performance and I didn't want to give in and give up but felt I was forced to make a stand. So, I picked up my bag, left the room and walked out towards the lift.

Suddenly, she was beside me and shouting in my face, stupid comments like, "I did it to get the best out of you. I know you will be good, and it will all be down to my direction." Malcolm was close behind her. He asked that I come back, and all would be fine. I noticed panic in her eyes; she had gone too far. She then apologised but in a half-hearted way. The rest of the rehearsals went without any problems, but she refused to give me any notes and ignored anything I said, thus leaving me with no positive direction. On transmission night she went around the whole cast giving them last-minute notes. Then she just looked at me and said, "I am going to pray for you." She had to have the last word. Derek came to see the show from the technical box. After it was all over, we went with the cast to have a drink. The producer and crew were already there, congratulating us on our performances. Valerie came into the bar, walked over to me and said, "You see, darling, all that I did made it work in your favour." Derek, always quite strong and opinionated, told her she was lucky to have me, that my performance was nothing to do with her, and that I pulled it off despite her. She simpered and said, "Oh, I really want you to play a part in my next project."

Derek simply said, "Over my dead body!" Happily, I got rather good reviews for that play. It is a fallacy to say that directors should be dictatorial. The fact is that all actors have insecurities, and most actors excel with praise and encouragement. I am glad to say that she was the only bad director I ever had.

In 1967 we looked for a bigger house and a very soon found the house that I still live in today. It's a converted pub in Old Windsor, and as soon as we entered it we were so taken by the character and the warm friendly atmosphere that without hesitation we made an offer and moved in. Eight thousand five hundred pounds was the price we paid. This meant we had to increase our mortgage payments, but at this time we were both doing well professionally and so it was easily affordable. Commercial television was expanding rapidly, becoming more and more competitive with the BBC. Advertising revenue was enabling commercial stations to make bigger and better dramas and spectacular variety shows. For a time, it was not deemed good for serious actors to appear in short commercials, but as time went by, actors realised that just one commercial could keep you alive for a year. Alongside the fees and the royalties, your face could become so well known it could help your career to flourish. As a child, still at school, my fellow pupils and I often appeared in commercials for ice cream and cereals for the Pearl & Dean company for showing in cinemas.

Once, my agent sent me to audition for a commercial company based in an office off the Harrow Road in North West London. The company was run by two brothers, Ridley and Tony Scott from the north of England. So creative was their work they were the first company to go to if you wanted your product to be noticed.

All their commercials were mini masterpieces. My first commercial after I became a mother was for Fairy Liquid. The storyline was about a young mother and a pre-school child. It was such a success that a couple of years later I did another Fairy Liquid commercial with a different child. I also made a commercial for Findus Fish with Ridley. Here, the storyline was that a young couple were on their honeymoon in Brixham, Devon. It was February and cold and misty. We were there for days, wandering along the beach while Ridley was filming from a cliff well above. Today it would be a lot cheaper to use a drone. We then spent two days on a studio set with me dishing up a plate of fish with dry ice creating steam above. How much must that have cost to make, I wonder. Another commercial I did was for Marmite. This was an elaborate storyline about three different stages in my character's life. I started off as a teenager then moved on to being a hippy chick before ending up with a family. This commercial had the by-line "Marmite the growing up spread you never grow out of." I could hardly believe it when an envelope arrived with a cheque in it for six thousand pounds. That was a great deal of money in the late 1970s, so I bought a new car for the very first time.

Not long after that, I got a call to do three episodes in a series about a London street market, called *Honey Lane*. The series was based in Soho in a street market. My old friend and colleague, Gerry Mill, was the director. I first met him on *The Rag Trade*. Gerry was a lovely man, very intelligent with a laid-back attitude to work. (Later, in the 1980s, I did two episodes on *Crown Court* for Gerry. The rehearsals were so casual: they finished at one, and we all went to Gerry's club to drink the afternoon away. I only did that once, as I nearly fell down the stairs and don't remember getting home, let alone learning my lines.)

Rehearsals and filming days were easy and stress-free. I played Dawn, a Soho stripper! See how far I had come with my regional accents! I only had a couple of scenes, but the writers decided to write me in as a full-time cast member. It was a good job and paid well at the time, so I employed au pairs to look after Sarah. Then, at age three, she started to go to a play school three days a week. *Honey Lane* was great job, and we had quite a young cast: Ian Gregory, Ray Lonnen, and Jane Blackburn.

Honey Lane

The cast socialised a lot together and we enjoyed some great parties at our new house. It was during the late sixties hippy era and there was great music and clothes that were fun. We were all casual and carefree. Janey and her friends had introduced me to marijuana, and I really liked the effect it had on me, as it usually made me hysterical with laughter. Fortunately, I don't appear to have inherited my father's addictive personality; basically, I can take it or leave it. We had a lean-to greenhouse out the back of our house, and someone gave me some marijuana seeds which grew to an enormous height of at least two metres. However, once matured, I had absolutely no idea how to process it. My friend Janey suggested it might be an idea to dry it slowly in the oven, stalks, seeds and all, then blend it into a herb type of substance, ready to roll with tobacco. There was no internet or YouTube sites in those days to give advice. So, I put it all into a large plastic tub and, just in case I got a visit from the police, I marked it "Parsley". Many years later, my daughter

Sarah used some in a recipe for the dish "Cod in Parsley Sauce" for her O-level cookery exam. The nuns at her convent school thought it was delicious and gave her an A! I became a bit wild in my mid-twenties. It wasn't the drugs or alcohol; it was, I think, because I had grown up very fast and had no time during my teenage years to be young, irresponsible, and carefree. Derek was away a great deal during that time, and we were growing apart and leading very separate lives.

Then came the summer of free love and a complete change in relationships along with a freedom of expression. I am afraid to say I was quite wild and an outrageous flirt. This is difficult for me to admit, knowing my daughter will finally learn that her mother was, at times, a bit of a slut! But if you are going to write your life story, it has to include warts and all. Derek and I never ever referred to our lives when we were apart, but when he was at home, we both behaved impeccably. As the old saying goes, "What goes on location, stays on location." Just once, I caught him having an affair with a well-known actress, but how could I be judgemental when I was not an angel myself? When you are young and attractive and constantly in the public eye, it is easy with new-found fame to believe anything is acceptable. I met many well-known stars from film and music, but I don't want to name and shame anyone. Suffice to say, nothing, and no one, ever tempted me to jeopardise the happiness of my beloved daughter and my family's security. As far as I was concerned, flirting was just a bit of fun. One of my admirers was a young Russian prince who was the former boyfriend of Brigitte Bardot. He was spectacularly good-looking: long blond hair, ripped jeans, and silk scarves wrapped round his slim hips. He had a great Russian accent and was a friend of Janey, who knew many society people. Anyway, it was lust at first sight, and we spent a couple of days together but, as usual, after a time I tired of him. He then accused me of treating him like a bellboy, which made me feel rather guilty. Luckily, Derek and I had such a special bond we both survived our escapades and grew very close as we got older.

I decided to make it a priority to be with Derek whenever possible and travelled to some wonderfully exotic locations, taking Sarah out of school whenever I could. My career suffered, as I turned down work that would have been good. It wasn't a problem though since I had been working solidly in the business since the age of twelve. It was twenty-five years on, and my ambition had dimmed somewhat anyway. I regret it now, as I love acting and deep down would still like to do it again.

I am not generally very sociable with people if I believe we would not have anything in common. That sounds as though I am stand-offish. I am not at all like that, but I don't see the point in spending time talking about subjects in which I have no interest. It would be easy to assume that I am unfriendly, when in fact I am more interested in other people's lives than my own. We usually make friends for life in the first twenty-five years of life, but just sometimes people come into your life later and with whom you immediately click.

Around this time, I met two new friends, who lived in Old Windsor, for the first time: Hilary Matthews and Dee St George York. Because of my working life, I had very few friends outside of the entertainment industry. Hilly and Dee where totally different, as both had travelled extensively and both had experienced acting. Dee had performed in Dublin and Hilly was a former RADA student. So, in essence, we were compatible. That may sound a little patronising, but I crave the company of eccentrics and especially those eccentric friends who share my sense of humour and make me laugh. Hilly and Dee had both these qualities. We all had young school-age children and were looking for something to do between jobs and childcare. We decided, along with Kate Cooper, my first Windsor friend, to form a company that would do anything from child-minding to catering. Over the next two years we worked hard and named the company Problems Unlimited. You can imagine some of the more unusual requests we had.

The most surprising was to provide a sheep for slaughter to a Muslim family who had recently moved into a large house in

Old Windsor. We were unaware of the horrible sacrifice procedure that was a standard cultural ritual. The people concerned told us the sheep was for the children to have as a pet. It was only during our research that we discovered from a sheep breeding farmer what was to happen. When we confronted the chap we were dealing with, he announced that he would be happy to give the meat to the poor people of Old Windsor! As if that would make a difference! Then he offered us even more money than he had done originally. I'm sure the family eventually found someone to comply with their request, and for the right price. Although being simple family cooks, we took all sorts of catering jobs for weddings, christenings and for many parties and got away with it! One job was to cater for the opening of a new wholesale freezer centre attended by four hundred butchers and their wives. They requested hot soup, sausage rolls, chicken and ham vol-au-vents and sandwiches. We had an early start on a Monday morning and employed the kids to help. They were filling the vol-au-vents with the chopped ingredients in white sauce, but unfortunately we ran out of filling for fifty people. Hilary scavenged through her fridge and, voila, she came up with some left-over swede and carrot mash from her Sunday lunch. We doused it in soy sauce and labelled those fifty as vegetarian! For a butchers' event?

There were other jobs that were not so appealing, like cleaning out a toilet in a minicab office and scrubbing an empty swimming pool while the glamorous owner sat on the side with a gin and tonic. We managed to keep going, however, and made a few bob (shillings) to supplement our income.

We had started having holidays in Majorca at a little cove called Cala Vinas. We stayed in a Forte hotel, the Cala Vinas. It was well away from the packed tourist areas like Magaluf. While sitting on the beach one day listening to Neil Diamond, we were approached by a couple who were sitting nearby. They asked us if we would mind their children, Jane and John, while they took a trip on their yacht. They were with another couple, Arthur and Pat Snipe, and their two adopted sons. We watched them go off in a Riva sports boat then board a Nicholson yacht further out in the harbour. The couple were Pat and Dave Whelan. Dave had been a professional footballer but had broken his leg at Wembley. He became a very successful businessman with his chain of JJB Sports shops and being the owner of Wigan Football Club.

Problems Unlimited

They were lovely, down-to-earth northerners with whom, I am happy to say, we remain in touch after forty-five years. We have spent many happy evenings in their beautiful Barbados home, Maddox, surrounded by their old friends whom we call the Wigganers!

The other family, Arthur and Pat Snipe, had made their fortune when Arthur was a young engineering student and his father worked in a coal mine. His father asked him to design machinery to gouge out coal from the face of the mine. His idea took off and he became a millionaire from the patent of that design. It is always amazing to hear success stories like these from simple working class families.

THE FIRST BOND FILM

In the autumn of 1972, I got a call from Derek, who was on location in New Orleans with *Live and Let Die*, the first Bond film with Roger Moore. Derek suggested that I come out to join him with Sarah. Of course, I wanted to go and managed to get Sarah out of school provided I took her schoolbooks with us. What a wonderful experience it was to join this great crew headed by Cubby Broccoli and Harry Saltzman, the producers of all the Bond films, and director Guy Hamilton, with whom Derek went on to make very many other films. Roger Moore was a delight and had already palled up with Derek, having the same sense of humour.

New Orleans in those days was still rather raw, and there was a great deal of racial tension. Our apartment was in the French Quarter, and it was quite common to hear gunshots at night. One night, when we were coming home, there were cops all over the place, hiding behind buildings and firing shots. It felt like we were on a gangster film set, or in an episode of *Law & Order*. One of the locations was in a rather remote area on the bayou (waterways and swamp land). The scene was a jet boat water chase between Bond and the baddies. The director chose a particular house, an old colonial southern mansion straight out of *Gone with the Wind*, where the occupants were supposedly having a wedding feast in the grounds of the building. The action was for one of the jet boats in the film to crash straight into the wedding cake, with the bride bursting into tears.

We got to know the family very well and had many happy times in their house in Slidell, a suburb of New Orleans the other side of Lake Pontchartrain. They loved to entertain us all, but the lady of the house had never cooked. So, Kalista Henricks, another location wife, and I bought all the ingredients and cooked for the family and for the whole crew. We are still in touch with the family today and have been back a few times to stay in that wonderful mansion.

The film then moved to a new location, Jamaica. As the producers had hired a charter plane, Sarah and I and other crew families moved with them. We stayed in an amazing hotel called the Sans Souci in Ocho Rios. This location was also used in some of the scenes. Our days there were spent happily sunbathing, swimming, and dining on amazing meals. It was so luxurious we even had a maid allocated to our little two-bedroom bungalow. It is very easy to become accustomed to this lifestyle, but we were not in the income bracket that could support it.

Whilst all this may sound like a travel brochure, the reality was that it was just another wonderful place to make a film. We often had dinner with Roger and Louisa Moore and their children, Deborah and Geoffrey. Sarah was a year younger than Deborah and they got on very well together.

One hot afternoon, when we were dozing in chairs around the pool, we overheard a conversation between the two little girls. It went something like this.

Deborah: "My daddy is so rich we can buy anything we want."

Sarah: "Is he? Well, my mother is very poor. She even has to borrow money from the bank!" Deborah, thoughtfully: "Well, you know, the more I think about it, my daddy isn't really that rich; in fact, he is probably quite poor too." There was, of course, some smothered laughter over this. I don't know if it seemed cooler to be poor and that's why Deborah changed her story, or if in fact she felt sorry for Sarah and backtracked to make her feel more comfortable.

Roger was one of the nicest and funniest actors around and so self-deprecating about how lucky he was. Sometimes he said things like, "I will get found out one day!" He was still a complete professional in every film he made. Another anecdote arose from when he was working in Rhodes on a film called *Escape to Athena*, in which he was playing a German commandant. I asked him what accent he was using and his answer was, "Oh, my usual Streatham." He is sadly missed by so many people.

Mum, Dad, Roger Moore

Derek went straight from *Live and Let Die* to making a film called *The Tamarind Seed* with Julie Andrews in glorious Barbados, the first of our many visits to this island. The actor, Omar Sharif, was such a gentleman and a ladies' man and liked to hang out with the crew. He and Derek got on well and kept in touch when we got back. He also asked if Derek could work on his next film, to be made in Montreal, Canada. It was a low-budget children's film about Benjy, a well-trained dog, and I flew out to Montreal for a week. The guys were bored, so every night they went to a stadium to watch and to bet on trotting races. I was proud to be the only female allowed to join them. Omar organised an amazing table piled high with the most expensive caviar, smoked salmon, champagne and other expensive food and wine. A woman would come to take our bets and collect the money. We never had to move a muscle, as she organised everything. Omar would bet on practically every rider and won consistently. He was a well-known gambler: backgammon, blackjack, he did it all.

One night it was getting late, and he called the woman over to collect his winnings. She paid him out, but he wasn't satisfied, and I witnessed another side to him that I found quite shocking. He stood up, slapped her and knocked her to the floor.

We were all stunned but realised that this would be a bad situation if it wasn't resolved quickly. So, we helped her up and got her some medical assistance, then called a cab and were able to smuggle Omar out of the back door of the stadium to avoid the paparazzi. How could a charming, funny, generous man turn into such a bully? I hope he paid her some compensation, but regardless, my opinion of him changed that night.

Sarah studied at the Marist, a Catholic convent school well known for having a high standard of education and having had many students reach Oxbridge entry with their school results. Sarah was a good student and always in the top ten in her class. One day, quite out of the blue, she said she didn't want to stay on at school, as she wanted to be an actress and go to a stage school. Oh! History repeating itself. This time, though, we felt that due to her good grades at school it would be crazy to take her out at the age of twelve and move her into a completely different environment. We tried to persuade her that she could audition for all the adult drama schools, but she was determined and did some quite drastic things to prove her point - including disruptive behaviour at school. I eventually took her back to my mother's house and had a good discussion. It was my wise old mum who said we should let her go to stage school, because she and my father had allowed me to go, and I had done all right. Well, of course, what could we say? Sarah attended the Italia Conti school in Clapham for a couple of years and then did a very brave thing. She realised that changing schools had been a big mistake and she asked to go back to the Marist School.

A RELUCTANT MANAGER/ROADIE/FUNDER

Sarah still wanted to pursue a career in the entertainment business so decided not to try for university but do a course in psychology at Windsor College to finish her schooling. While there, she met up with some Windsor boys and formed a band called The Worried Parachutes. This seemed to me to be a harmless hobby for the time being. I watched them rehearse a couple of times and I must say that even as a mum, I was quite impressed with her musicality and performance. We had a lot of fun, with me driving the band around and generally helping out. Eventually though, they ended up under the very professional eye of David Enthoven, who then managed the band Squeeze, and also Emerson, Lake & Palmer! This was all a strange learning curve for me, having to be on the other side, but it was certainly a very different business to be in. The pop industry was full of rogues and empty promises. I soon learnt the ropes, however, and eventually took on other acts. Sarah's early band fell apart following arguments, disappointments, and big musical differences. She has her own story to tell, so I won't dwell on the different routes she took at that time, (including a year's course at the Actors Studio, London) without ever having a clear game plan. I was now deeply involved with the music business and let all my acting work opportunities go, much to the disappointment of my then agent, Terry Carney.

Derek and I decided to give the band a hand and so we booked a concert hall for them in which they could perform a gig for people we knew in the music business. We sent out invitations to all and sundry and then let them show what they could do.

They had original songs written by the band of fifteen-year-olds, with a nod to Siouxsie and the Banshees, Adam and the Ants and others in that "New Romantic" style. Most exciting of all though was that Sarah shone like the pop star she was to become later.

I was nominated to look after the band, bearing in mind they were very young and needed a driver, roadie, agent, and manager, not to mention funder, which of course any parent would do.

In the summer of 1983, the band was booked to play some London dates so they could be seen by people in the industry. The first time I met George Michael and Andrew Ridgeley from Wham! was at the Clarendon Hotel in Hammersmith, about that time. This was a very run-down art deco hotel on the Broadway that housed a basement rock venue for young bands. It was my first experience in managing a young pop band. The Worried Parachutes had recently been recording some tracks for a new record company, Innervision Records, a subsidiary label of CBS records, whose first signing was Wham!. The company invited Wham! down to see us perform. George and Andrew were very enthusiastic, and George was dancing on a table amongst the crowd. Their A&R man handed me a white label record of one of their first singles, "Wham Rap!". I played it later to my band and they all said, "It won't do well; rap is out." In fact, they went on to make history and sell more than twenty million records. I still have that white label record. Sadly, George passed away on Christmas Day 2016 at the young age of fifty-three. That was the same year that we lost David Bowie and Rick Parfitt, two other rock legends. The Worried Parachutes eventually fragmented and split up but having gained a lot of experience after playing so many gigs. The bass player from the band was a lovely, talented boy called Mick Bund.

Mick Had a unique song writing talent. He and Sarah formed a duo called Prime Time, which went on to build quite a following. They used to rehearse at a large studio complex called Easy Hire, which is where they met producer Tom Newman, who had produced the studio album *Tubular Bells* by Mike Oldfield. Tom decided to take them on and produce some tracks, after many gigs and winning the Radio London Best Band prize. A trip to New Orleans where they enlisted two American boys Rod and Danny Chauvin, and they finally called it a day.

picture of Mick Bund

Mick then formed a rock band called Mexico 70, for which I was now the manager, having earned my stripes over two years. Mick and Sarah were very close, like brother and sister, and Derek and I always thought of Mick as the son we never had.

There was now so much happening with the artists – Mick with his new band and me as manager. Then I took on a new female singer called Janey Lee Grace, who has gone on to be a successful radio presenter and bestselling lifestyle author, promoting products that are natural and healthy and a series of books where the titles are prefaced by the word "Imperfectly".

Sarah, having finished an acting course in London, began to work with other musicians and, through various contacts, became the lead singer in the band Saint Etienne.

I was living an interesting life promoting new talent and enjoying wonderful holidays and trips with Derek. He went on to make one more James Bond film: after *Diamonds Are Forever* and *Live And Let Die it* was *The Man With The Golden Gun* set in Thailand. Sometimes you were able to buy clothes from the wardrobe department. Derek made an offer for a spectacular dress that was worn by Jill St. John, in Diamonds Are Forever. It was a tiny size eight, so not many people could get into it. Fortunately, I managed to squeeze into it, then Sarah wore it in a pop video for "Hug My Soul".

Janey Lee Grace

Sarah in Bond Dress

Julie in Bond Dress

FIRST SPANISH HOME

My mother had decided to sell the family holiday home in Burnham-on-Crouch, and the proceeds from the sale would go to us, the four children. With my quarter share, I decided to buy a small flat in an area of southern Spain where we had started to spend a lot of time, Guadalmina, near San Pedro in the beautiful area of Andalusia.

Sarah, and her friend Carol, came out to Spain, and we stayed with my friend Kate, who had moved there some years before. We found a darling little one-bedroom flat, south-facing and in a very beautiful location close to the sea. We were so excited about this little flat.

Derek had been away filming when I bought it, so I was filled with trepidation to see if he would be as happy as I was with our little home from home. So, after Derek finished his latest film, we decided to drive down to the south of Spain, bringing with us all sorts of items: linen, towels and kitchen equipment we would need to equip the flat.

We drove through France, stopping for one night to stay at a beautiful little chateau. Then on through Bordeaux to Spain, staying in Paradores. These are heritage buildings that were turned into hotels, some of which date back to the sixteenth century. I remember an old monastery on the south side of Madrid, with a fountain in the courtyard and a bell tower.

We would drive from nine a.m. until around four p.m., when it got too hot to drive any further, as it was August, and our Volvo did not have any air conditioning. We would have a swim and a nap and then go in for dinner. Finally, our last journey took us south over the Sierra Nevada mountain range, down to Malaga.

We had already booked an appointment with a solicitor to finalise the paperwork and pick up the keys. The flat had previously been owned by an elderly Swedish lady and had been decorated in a rather grim Scandinavian style with dark rustic wood and was full of textile wall hangings and rugs. This part of the world, however, has a beautiful, warm, peachy light that lends itself to pastels and light white furniture. Derek had been paid some dollars for directing a fight scene in his last film, so we decided to use that to refurbish the flat.

We hired an English plumber-builder, Denis, to do the work. We allowed him to use the garage to store his machinery in exchange for a good rate. We ripped out the galley kitchen and made the entire apartment open plan except for the large double bedroom and bathroom. We had a tiny balcony facing the sea, just big enough to take a table and two chairs to sit out at night and listen to the crickets, look at the sea, and watch the lights come on in the fishing boats out to sea.

For us, this was a small paradise. We had a handyman, Antonio, who was the janitor in charge of the complex, and there was also the big bonus for Derek of having many golf courses on our doorstep. For anyone who might be thinking of buying a holiday home in Spain, a note of warning: the Spanish authorities are extremely thorough regarding rules and regulations, fully trained in rubber-stamping, and champion staplers. Just one example of how frustrating such an obsession can be: in our lovely brand-new bijou flat, the only thing missing was a means of communication. There were no satellites for mobile phones yet and, in 1991, certainly no wifi. So, if you wished to contact your loved ones at home, you had to visit La Casa Telefonica, a small building in the middle of San Pedro, where there were booths with a telephone in each, and an operator at a desk who would make the call for you then patch it through. You then paid for the cost of the call in pesetas at the end.

We thought that to have a home phone installed would be wonderful, and our first visit to the telephone department in Marbella, half an hour away, went something like this. On entry, you collected a numbered ticket, say number fifty. This meant there were fifty people before you. Now, you sat and waited for half an hour with your address and passport ready for identification. Finally, a conversation went something like this.

"I wish to order a home phone for our new apartment."

"Si. Have you got ID?"

"Yes, here is my passport."

"Do you have your escritoire (deeds)? No? Sorry, you have to come back."

The following day, me talking. "Good morning. I would like to order a home telephone for our apartment."

"Si. Do you have an NIE number?"

Me. "Que?" Now it is the third day, and I am armed with all the requirements. "Hello, it's me again. I need to order a home telephone." I am fully prepared, armed with deeds, NIE number, passport.

"Si señorita." Then, the jobsworth brings out five pages of a contract. I sign all of them, and each one is rubber-stamped then stapled neatly together. Then, he looks at me and says, "What colour would you like? Blanco? It will be delivered to your address soon."

"Muchas gracias señor." I was so excited, but in ten years, it never turned up.

On the way back to England, we decided to cut out France and return via Santander, a port where you can catch an overnight ferry to Southampton. The trip across the Bay of Biscay was very rough and Derek, poor thing, suffered badly with sea sickness.

Derek started work on a film, with actor John Goodman, called *King Ralph*. The story was about a distant relative of the Queen, who inherits the throne after an electrical accident kills off all the royal family. This was to be Derek's very last film. It was Christmas 1990, and our old friend, Al Mitchell, invited us to Christmas lunch at his home in Richmond. There was a nice group of our old mates, including Richard O'Sullivan and his wife Christine, and Shirin Taylor, a wonderfully eccentric actress.

After lunch, Derek said he wanted to go for a walk, as the meal had made him feel very bloated. As we walked down towards the river, I suddenly noticed that he was looking particularly tired and pale. I assumed this was due to his last film, which he had only just finished and on which a difficult situation had arisen, with the director being rather paranoid.

On New Year's Eve we were invited to our friend Shona's house. It was close by, and we sauntered down there at about nine o'clock. Derek again said he was not feeling too well. One of our old friends, Dr Steve Culling, was at the party, and Derek had a quiet word with him about his symptoms: pain in the left-hand side of his abdomen, fatigue, and a bloated stomach. Steve looked concerned and advised Derek to go to see his own doctor first thing after the New Year break.

Somehow, I knew in my heart that this was serious, I insisted on going in to see the doctor with him, just to be able to remember everything he said. Initially, the doctor felt a lump close to Derek's liver. From the look in his eyes, he was clearly thinking the worst. We knew all our doctors in those days, and Sarah had gone to school with this doctor's daughter. Fortunately, we had been paying into Bupa for many years, as my mother felt that the NHS should be for poor people and not for people who were able to pay for health insurance. Derek was admitted into The Princess Margaret Hospital for tests and diagnosed with pancreatic cancer within the week. Even with the early diagnosis, his prognosis was not good. We were told that he should put his affairs in order and that he would need an operation to bypass the pancreas immediately. I was very angry and fretful, feeling that no one should give someone a "die by date", as that can take away hope that may keep a sick patient alive or prolong life longer than expected. I wrote a scathing letter to the surgeon who treated him, explaining that unless you know the patient, you should tread carefully about how you approach the subject of terminal cancer. After the operation, the doctor referred Derek to an oncologist at Hammersmith Hospital. The department was full of hopeful and enthusiastic scientists all striving to find a cure. They treated Derek as a patient who deserved to live, and determined they were going to do their very best to help him. At last, he now felt a glimmer of optimism and that someone was rooting for him and not writing him off as a hopeless case. The chemotherapy was gruelling and debilitating with terrible side effects such as sickness and lethargy, but we told ourselves that they would not be treating him if they thought there was no chance of him surviving. His friends phoned all the time to see how he was, and I was instructed to say that he had a gall bladder problem, as he did not want colleagues in the film business to know more than that, in case he should be able to work later.

Sadly, he never felt well enough to lead a normal life, and the morphine that was prescribed rendered him weak and sleepy. Weeks went by with a routine of chemotherapy then a rest. I would research alternative treatments and seek out healers who, although they may not have been able to save him, made him feel a whole lot better.

We also had regular visits from the wonderful Marie Curie nurses. They were angels, always so cheerful and spending hours talking to Derek. I am still in touch today with Jean Horwood, one of those nurses.

One day in April, the sun was coming out and we both went into the garden, me to do a bit of weeding and Derek to sit in the sun. That night he developed a cough from a chest infection, got up to go to the toilet and fell onto the floor. I tried desperately to help him up and finally managed to get him back into bed. The next morning, the doctor called an ambulance and had him admitted to Hammersmith Hospital. The doctor who saw him first examined him and then after reading his notes, put him straight back onto intravenous chemotherapy. In his case, the tumour was decreasing, but his body was too weak to go on. He was winning the battle but losing the war.

Many caring people assured me that there is life after death, and I can only say what I personally feel. Yes, I truly think we do go on, and I feel very sad for people who believe we have no soul and no future. If you are never going to see your loved ones again, the big question remains: What on earth are we here for? I was staying with our friends Al and Sonia, as they lived close to the hospital. One night I got a call at two a.m. to say that Derek was asking for me. The nurse felt that he didn't have very long to go, so I called Sarah and Michele, Derek's sister, who then passed the message on to Derek's brothers and sister Robin, Gordon and the rest of the family.

Derek was conscious for a good length of time, chatting to us all as the rest of his family arrived. I didn't want to alarm him, or them, as it was still only five a.m. in the morning on that 4th May. I remember hearing him talking to someone in his half-sleep, and when I asked who he was speaking to, he said Bobby Murrell was there. Bobby had died many years before. We discussed having a holiday in Barbados, saying that we should go there again, as we had spent such lovely times there in the past. He really liked the island, and we thought perhaps the sun would help heal him.

Neither of us wanted to face the real truth; it was too painful to bear. So, we carried on as before, telling each other that he would be going home soon to get over the chemotherapy. Again,

I felt it was important to keep his hopes up, as no one really wants to know they are dying. While Sarah, Michele, and I sat with him, he finally took his last breath, and I knew he had gone. There was a sense of relief, for as sad as I was, I did not want him to suffer any more and knew that he was now free from pain.

DEREK'S CAREER

I need to add a few anecdotes about Derek's career. Derek was a very well-respected first assistant director. Sometimes, he had to work with difficult and inexperienced directors, and occasionally, diplomacy would fly out of the window. One memorable time was on the film *A Clockwork Orange*, an iconic film directed by Stanley Kubrick. His relationship with Stanley was normally very good, as he had worked with him previously on *2001: A Space Odyssey*. At that time, they had got on famously and Derek and I had spent some time socially at Stanley's house with his family. Stanley was an idiosyncratic, temperamental artist with a vision that must be obeyed. On this day, they were working late in a tower block, ten storeys up in a cramped council flat on a London "sink" estate. The crew were tired and weary after shooting for many days and nights and into overtime. Stanley kept himself going with a selection of prescription drugs and pills to keep him alert, so he had an advantage over the rest of the crew and company.

He decided that the scene needed more light coming in from the window and, as it was dark, this proved to be quite complicated. Derek mentioned that to erect a lamp ten storeys up the side of a building was probably impossible without scaffolding. In his frustration, Stanley told Derek to piss off.

Having had more than enough for the night, Derek collected his bags and left. The next morning, all hell broke loose, as he told me he was not going back on the set and that I was not to answer the phone, which rang constantly. Eventually, a posse from the studio turned up on the doorstep and demanded to speak to him. They begged him to come back, as they knew that no one else could handle Stanley as well as Derek. Then a letter of apology came through the door. So, reluctantly he went back to work for the last few days of the shoot. Sad to say, he never worked with Stanley again, but by this time, of course, the bush telegraph had spread news of the disagreement half-way around the world. I still have that very nice apology letter from Stanley to Derek.

Another incident took place in 1986 on a well-known film, *Aliens*. The director, James Cameron, was a hard taskmaster and made many demands. He was married to one of the producers, Gale Anne Hurd, who had never had any practical experience in filming and spent most of her time shopping in Harrods. There was a young child in the film, Carrie Henn (we are still in touch today), and being a minor, she had to have regulated hours of work and was not allowed to work overtime. Unfortunately, the director decided to ignore the rules and insisted she stay longer on set to get a certain shot. Finally, Derek did what all good assistant directors do and dismissed Carrie to go home. James Cameron was so furious he screamed at Derek, who by this time had gone to the production office. He was then asked to go to the producer's office, where Gale calmly announced, "We are going to have to let you go," and that he was fired.

Derek then told her that she had not earned the right to fire him, and that he was resigning anyway. Derek then felt it was right to address the crew, whom he knew well, having worked with them on many previous films. The following morning, Julian Wall, his second assistant, and Melvin Lind, his third assistant, called the crew in early. Derek arrived, went onto the set where they were all assembled and explained his position. Then, he left and came home. There followed uproar at Pinewood! An emergency meeting was held with the other producers and the director, during which time the crew, led by the wonderful Sigourney Weaver, decided to come out on strike until Derek was re-instated. No one remembers that ever happening in film before, but Derek had such a huge reputation for being the best and most considerate first assistant director in the industry, and everyone had more respect for him than for the director and they all stood by him.

At home, the phone rang continually, and I was told not to answer it. Finally, there was a knock on the door and the main producer, Walter Hill, and the production supervisor came in and told Derek about the strike and asked him to please come back. Derek said he would return, on the condition that he got an apology from Gale Anne Hurd and James Cameron, which he did. There was a big round of applause as he walked onto the set. There is an account of what happened on the film on Netflix, but the truth was not recorded properly and has left out the strike. Well, I was there and so were his assistants, and they would confirm this version, as I have reported it, is true.

SINGLE WORKING WOMAN

I had moved in with my mother, as the plan was to have Derek in her bungalow, which was without stairs for him to climb, and to have both of us to care for him. Having my mother with me at that time was probably why I coped as well as I did. She took me back to my teenage years and nurtured me like a child. The funeral was arranged by a lot of very close friends, who are still close today. Garth and Hilli dealt with all the legal details; Janey Lee Grace, being a practising Christian, spoke to the vicar about the service hymns and music. Julian Wall and Melvin Lind, Derek's film assistants, booked Pinewood Studios for the funeral wake.

What an amazing turnout there was both for the service and for the wake. Derek would have been so touched to see everyone who came to say goodbye. All his colleagues in the film business were there; some had even flown in from other foreign locations. I was surviving on champagne and temazepam and was amazed at how many names I remembered of his work colleagues – or was Derek whispering in my ear? I got a message halfway through the wake from Lord Grade, a well-known producer, who said he was a great admirer of Derek's work, and he would like to pay the bill for the funeral and wake. I was truly amazed and thanked him profusely. The message came just before we opened another crate of champagne. We opened it, nonetheless. I wanted to make sure Derek had the best funeral ever. I have kept a scrapbook with all the amazing letters I received from his friends and colleagues. It is something, along with all the films and scripts I have, that I hope will one day will be of interest to our grandsons, Spencer and Sam Kelly, both now entering the entertainment business in music and film.

We had a district nurse who used to visit and administer his doses of morphine. She was a strict Catholic and prayed for him often. She came to visit me after his death and suggested she could arrange a Mass to be said for him, as she had grown to like him very much over the months. A few of us attended, and though it was very solemn, it gave us final closure on his life. She turned to me after the Mass and said, "You see, Julie, he had to die now, in order to come back and save the world." Wow! I didn't think Catholics believed in reincarnation.

I look back now to myself at the age of just forty-five and realise how young I was to be a widow. I am, by nature, a happy and
optimistic person so knew I had to get on with my life. My management company was beginning to do well, and all my artists
had record deals. Two weeks after Derek died, Janey Lee Grace
was number two in the pop charts and on *Top of the Pops*, Sarah's
first Saint Etienne single was out, and Mick of Mexico 70 had
signed to a small indie label, Cherry Red Records in the UK and
Big Pop in Philadelphia. I was too busy to grieve, though I had
probably done most of my grieving over Derek's final six months
and the last weeks of his life, so I just got on with life, occasionally breaking down in tears if something reminded me of him.
Janey was a thoroughly professional artist, and we spent many
months on the road promoting her records, staying in draughty
B&Bs and eating in motorway cafes. Then suddenly, the success
of her Top Ten single, *7 Ways to Love*, catapulted her career into
TV appearances, with many lucrative live night-club personal appearances. She was innovative and brave enough to tackle any
situation, even to the extent of making up songs to please club
managers, as we had not enough material for an album. I would
collect the money all in cash at the end of each gig, and then Janey
and her musical partner would make a dash to the car before we
could be mugged! It was the 1990s "rave" culture, where promotors would hire a space and a superstar DJ then bring in current
Top Ten artists to perform their latest hits to a backing track.

There were some scary moments, as we were dealing with
hundreds of pounds in cash, all in pound notes from the takings,
which I had to count out in a makeshift office alongside some
very dodgy promotors. How easy it is now that bank transfers
mean you never even have to see the cash. We visited clubs in

Europe, but by this time, her success meant that we travelled in style and stayed in decent hotels.

Janey suggested I should take on the management of two very young girls from the popular teenage TV series *Byker Grove*, filmed in Newcastle. The series was based on a local youth club and the relationships between the kids. Ant and Dec (Anthony McPartlin and Declan Donnelly) started their career on that programme.

They were so popular they were snapped up by Telstar records and promoted as *PJ & Duncan*, their character names in the show. After doing the usual A&R meetings, including a meeting with Simon Cowell (who, by the way, was a sweet and helpful man), I joined forces with Tilly Rutherford, another music man and entrepreneur, and we managed to also secure a record deal with the same label as Ant and Dec – Telstar Records.

Crush

Donna Air and Jayni Hoy were labelled as the pop duo Crush. I had forgotten what it was like to chaperone two fifteen-year-old girls, as despite their obvious charm, they also could be treacherous, naughty and deceitful. They were a handful and were determined to have everything they wanted, as in *Byker Grove* they had been spoiled rotten.

In the music industry, managers and record companies turn perfectly pleasant and talented young teenagers into demanding monsters who never have to lift a finger. They are driven everywhere in a limousine, clothed by well-known fashion designers and given far too much money. They end up unable to make decisions for themselves or perform a simple task such as booking a table for dinner. They invariably develop enormous egos and a sense of entitlement, especially when they start out so young and have not really earned their success. Jayni was a sweet girl, slightly Latino-looking, dark puppy-dog eyes, and a curvaceous figure. Donna was quite the opposite: tall for her age with skinny legs, naturally blond hair and a Viking look about her. She had a perfect photogenic face. It was difficult to take your eyes off her. She was fun, naughty, but also quite sympathetic at times. We had children camping out on my doorstep just to get a glimpse of the pop duo, and the pair of them would nip outside to chat to the fans and sign autographs. They were well acquainted with fan worship, as they had appeared on TV twice a week for some years.

Life for them was based on just how much fun they could have. And why not, at that age? During their recording sessions and TV promotion work, they stayed with me, for to put them up in a hotel would have been disaster. I soon found out that at fourteen/fifteen, they were also sexually active, and both had boyfriends back in Newcastle. They were also accustomed to getting drunk and experimenting with drugs. Well, I thought, it's not my business to be judgemental or disapproving, as I was just the manager, but I did warn them about the potential consequences of their behaviour. I also tried to teach the girls something about managing their money, as they had been given a small advance from the record company.

This was merely pocket money to them, of course. The girls' parents were relying on me to keep them out of trouble, but I don't think they had any idea of just how much of a risk they were taking. Then, the inevitable happened. We had a night off and were sitting watching TV one evening, and one of them mentioned how large her breasts had become. At first, I assumed as she was still growing that it was just part of her physical development. However, when she went on to mention blue veins appearing, this set alarm bells ringing.

"Tell me truthfully: have you had unprotected sex?" I asked.

"Well, just the once," she replied.

"And when was your last period?" I continued.

"Well, I can't really remember," she said.

I went to the chemist to buy two pregnancy testing kits, just to make sure, hoping that the result would be negative. Then, having sent them both to the upstairs bathroom with clear instructions, I waited patiently. I heard a loud scream and raced upstairs to find the guilty one on her knees with the other one trying to pacify her. What happened next was carefully orchestrated by her mother, as I felt this was not my remit as a manager, especially as she was under-age. It was strategically arranged for them to have some time off with their families in Newcastle before promotion started on the next UK single release.

A termination in this case was probably the best outcome for everyone and a great relief all round. Whilst I tend to be against abortion, in this case, and as the girl was so young, I felt that had she continued with the pregnancy, it would have changed the whole course of her life simply because of one stupid mistake.

Times have changed however, and this would not be the case currently, for had she developed a sound career she could have got away with the pregnancy. Today, many actors/performers just build pregnancy into their schedules; in the case of our young singer, there was not enough back catalogue to retain the loyalty of fans. We continued with the promotion work as soon as she was fit and, during a trip to Spain to make a video, we all stayed (including the make-up artist) in our little flat in Guadalmina, and the promotional video was filmed in a luxurious house in Benahavís owned by Bill Curbishley, manager of The Who rock band. Promoting a new act and an album can take you all over the world, and, once the licensing deals had been done, off we went.

We started with a promo tour to of the USA, considering they had a single in the top thirty charts in Texas! The record was titled "Jelly Head". Our first stop was New York to do some press for the record company. It was 1996. While we were there, I was invited to meet the CEO of the Pyramid music agency, Sal Michaels, who had booked our promotional tour. Everyone will remember the amazing success of the all-girl group The Spice Girls. They were also in town, staying in Brooklyn. He told me confidentially that the girls were thinking of changing their management and would I be interested in taking them on? I said thank you for the offer, but I had enough problems with a girl duo as it was, and I didn't need another all-girl act giving me grief. I wonder how my life would have been if I had been accepted and taken on the job?

Next, we went to Japan, China, Indonesia, and other countries based in South-East Asia, as that was where the record releases took place.

We arrived in Jakarta at night after a very long flight from Hong Kong and were taken to a stunning hotel owned by the same person who appeared to own everything, including the night clubs and TV stations. He was a large man for an Asian and dressed and styled himself like Elvis Presley. We were tired. All we wanted was to go to our rooms for a shower and rest, but he had other ideas. "I have some drugs for the girls," he said, "then they won't be tired, and we can have some fun!" Whilst I was really shocked, I felt we really had no choice. So, we went for a meal in the hotel before being carted off to a huge night club.

Karaoke, and particularly ballads, were very big in this part of the world and there were booths arranged in the gallery for private parties. We were given glasses of champagne and then asked to choose a song to sing. I was told to choose a ballad that he and I could sing together. Blimey, I felt I had no choice, so I picked "True Love" from the film *High Society*. Thankfully, we didn't have cameras or recording devices on our phones, or selfies and other recordings would have ended up on YouTube!

Our next stop was Taiwan, where they had arranged for the girls to appear in a huge TV show that was broadcast throughout China. We arrived at the studio, and I heard the melody of their single "Jelly Head" being played.

Fear gripped me as I realised that they would be asked to sing live with a band, something they had never had to do before, and neither were they capable of doing so. We were given a two-minute sound check before the show started, and I knew we were in trouble. Miming covers up any mistakes, but live vocals truly reveal if you can, or cannot, sing.

Suddenly, the live audience filed in, the lights went up, and a miracle happened. On the side of the stage a filmy curtain caught fire from one of the lamps, and the audience made a dash for the exit. The fire was soon put out, but the minutes had ticked by. The producer came to apologise and explained that they would only be able to show the video recording. I thanked God profusely, and we went on our way.

Unexpectedly, we also had a hit record with the duo's first release, but there was not such a great response to the other tracks on the album.

We spent a great deal of time flying across the world, something I felt was a wonderful experience, as I visited so many different countries and cultures.

Jayni was an already seasoned traveller, having holidayed in many European countries, but Donna had come from a provincial working-class family and had never been to such exotic locations. I tried to engage the girls in a bit of a geography lesson, but they were generally not interested in where they were, just so long as there were shops, a nice hotel, and a pool if it was warm.

Sadly, the best-friend relationship Jayni and Donna had started to disintegrate. They each had separate friends in Newcastle, and they got fed up with each other. It is tough to be so young and so tired with never any time to be a teenager. It all became serious when we went to Ireland for a TV interview on a Belfast channel. Both girls had very curly hair, and their constant moan was how to get their hair straight. Anyone who has that problem knows exactly what water and humidity can do, as both turn a lovely, shiny bob into a pile of frizz.

We were having drinks in the green room after the show, and Donna was getting a bit tipsy. She started to flick water at Jayni, and Jayni, having the more explosive personality, threw a bottle of lager at her! Fortunately, this happened in a passage outside the green room, so no one saw it, but I felt it was time to go back to the hotel. Once we were in our rooms, mine opposite theirs, I suggested they order some sandwiches from room service. Unbeknown to me, they also ordered some drinks. Suddenly, Jayni was knocking loudly on my door. "Donna is attacking me," she shouted. I went across to their room to see what was going on and found that a physical fight had broken out just as the waiter arrived with a trolley of food. It was all such silly, childish stuff. The waiter's face was a picture as the two attractive young girls were wrestling in their underwear. Poor chap. He really didn't know where to look, and it became clear to me there was a real problem.

We returned to London for a break and the girls went back to see their parents. I had a good relationship with Donna and Jayni's mothers and had a long chat with them. The girls were tired of all the promotions and other work and wanted to spend more time with their boyfriends. The boyfriends, incidentally by this time, happened to be the bass player and drummer from the rock band that I managed, Mexico 70, after they had met up at my house one evening before the tour.

The record company had also become disenchanted with Crush and made it clear that they would probably not pick up the option of a second album but simply count their losses, which were huge. So many fail after the first album; it's a ruthless business. The cost of three videos and an album, loads of PR posters and other material can all mount up.

Donna wanted to change course and become a TV presenter. As a manager, I had no experience in this field, and Jayni wanted to fly to Australia with her boyfriend. I also felt that they should work out the rest of their record contract, but this wasn't to be, as they both decided to go their separate ways.

My position as their manager was therefore untenable. I had mixed feelings but was relieved not to be the minder and babysitter any longer. I had decided to join Mexico 70 on their tour of the USA and met their US record company in Philadelphia. Our tour manager, Charlie Brown, met me at the station and asked if I wanted the good news or the bad news. I opted for the bad news first. Our Winnebago had been stolen, complete with all our instruments and clothes. The good news was that the single had entered the billboard charts. Wow! I called the insurance company first, then my credit card provider, then took the band to a second-hand music store and replaced all the instruments.

The band was thrilled; they were like kids in a sweet shop. I then took them to a second-hand two-storey thrift shop, where they kitted themselves out with some quite outrageous clothes, Stetsons and an alligator suitcase.

I got a call from the record company to say the police had found the SUV, which the thieves had left on a hard shoulder off the freeway with the engine still running. They brought it back to the record company and stocked it up with petrol. Fortunately, we still had two guitars left in the under-storage area along with some T-shirts and CDs.

Entering the Holland Tunnel into New York city, the steering broke down. Poor Charlie was weaving into the wall and then back into the middle of the traffic until, at last, a cop on a bike turned up and we explained our predicament. He called ahead to a breakdown company which happened to be just outside the Holland Tunnel exit.

The band was playing at the Heeby-Jeebies club that night, after which we were heading to Upstate New York to stay with a fan who had a house in a small village. It was such a relief to get out of the city. Shortly after that, I left the tour in Maine and headed home.

Sadly, when we returned, there were issues within the band. Even though the tour had been quite successful, I lost Mexico 70, and twelve years of managing Mick Bund, whom we considered "family", was to come to an acrimonious end.

Mark Barret, whom we had hired as a guitarist, came to me one day and asked about publishing rights. I explained that the ownership of a music composition belonged to the person who wrote the top line melody and the lyrics; Mick Bund was the writer for Mexico 70. Mark was a good musician but not a creative writer.

He had no claim on the income from the song writer's share, therefore. It's all quite complicated and, in the past, there have been countless court cases in the pop music industry regarding who was responsible for making a song a hit. In some cases, a particular riff like, for instance, the saxophone introduction on Gerry Rafferty's big hit "Baker Street", was claimed to be a major contribution to the success of the song. Well, maybe it was, but there had to be a definitive rule. So, the saxophone player lost out in that case (although he was possibly awarded a percentage later).

I explained to Mark that it was not in my gift to give him a share of the publishing and that only Mick, the writer, could do that, and suggested he should sort it out with him. I think he turned against me at that point, poisoned the rest of the band against me, including Mick, who was very impressionable and easily swayed. I believe he convinced them that I was not doing enough for them but concentrating far too much on my other artists. The biggest problem, they felt, was that I was unable to get them a better record deal in the UK. The fact I had got them a deal in the biggest market in the world, the USA, plus a licensing deal in Europe, was apparently not enough. So, they decided they were going to manage themselves in the future, or rather that Mark was going to take over. I was devastated that Mick should be so disloyal after all that we, as a family, had done for him over a period of twelve years. We had treated him like one of the family, he having lived in my house for two years and writing his last album in my lounge. I think he regretted his behaviour later, as he had been pressured by the other band members, but by that time, I had lost all respect for him for being so weak. Unfortunately, after the last US tour, the US record company dropped them, and the band became fragmented. Mark became an alcoholic and died. Bass players came and went. Rick, the drummer, stayed loyal to Mick. However, after Mick's decline into drugs and alcohol abuse, he too moved on. I made my peace with Mick much later and tried desperately to help with his addiction, but he passed away in 2017, still fighting his demons. He had destroyed his physical and mental health and I no longer harbour hard feelings for him or have any regrets.

I knew in my heart that even though I had put Mexico 70 in front of every major record company in the UK, and although they had built up a small following, Mick did not have the stamina to succeed, and the music industry was never really that interested. There must be thousands of hopeful rock bands out there that have gone the same way as Mexico 70 and where the players have simply moved on with their lives.

Sarah was always very easy to manage and has never had an inflated opinion of herself. I think having been brought up in the entertainment business and spending much of her childhood on film and television sets mixing with all sorts of industry people, the whole stardom thing has never fazed her.

When I had stayed with Al and Sonia whilst Derek was in hospital, Al had arranged a night out at a restaurant in Richmond with some local friends. Actress Shirin Taylor, whom I had met before and who was currently in *Coronation Street*, and another actor friend lived locally. So, I decided to call on them and went round to Shirin and Adrian's house and knocked on the door. The door was opened by a familiar face. It was actor Johnny Wade. Johnny had had a small role in the TV series *Honey Lane*, and it was nice to see him again after so many years.

Sarah, Saint Etienne

We all went out for a meal, but it was difficult for me to let go, as I was anxious to get back to Derek, who was in hospital. This was three days before he died.

On New Year's Eve, eight months after Derek had died, Al had a party, and I was invited. Johnny Wade was also invited, and he asked me out on a date. I had already had the odd date but was not looking for anyone to replace my dearly beloved Derek. So, friends were my only companions. I decided I would go out with Johnny. It was nice going out with him, as we had a lot in common. But this was a time when he was looking for a more permanent partner, and I wasn't, so the relationship foundered.

We stopped seeing each other until three years later. I soon found that our rekindled relationship suited us both, as I was still working hard and travelling a great deal. So, we would meet up every Friday night and then Johnny would leave to return home each Monday morning. Johnny had been living a bachelor's life with his grown-up son, and I found it hard to accommodate someone permanently in my life after losing Derek.

But gradually we became closer. He was particularly warm and considerate to my mother, and she quickly absorbed him into the family, just as she had done with all my other friends. After ten years, Johnny moved in with me and, as I write this now, we are very much a loving couple. He is kind and supportive, and Sarah also loves him, which is something I am so happy about. It is good to see how well they get along. I believe fate takes a hand when you reach a crossroads in your life. I had become disenchanted with the music industry and with the new technology. The ability to stream any tracks meant that the industry took a dive from which it has never quite recovered. This digital change caused many people in the music industry to lose their jobs.

Out of the blue I got a call from my cousin, Joan, who asked me what I was doing and wondered if I would like to help her with a new musical production called *Moses*. I was happy to go along and help on the two workshop performances, as it gave me a new purpose in life. It was also like putting on an old, familiar glove to be working with trained actors again.

I had forgotten just how capable they were compared to the rough talent in the music business. Working with Joan was such a joy, as she is a very caring and considerate person and has a huge knowledge of the workings of theatre. I knew nothing about producing shows, having only acted out front on stage. Sometimes, in her early days, and through no fault of her own, she was a little gullible where the sharks in show business were concerned (but not any more). I had worked with the best and the worst so was aware of all the scams and tricks people do to get a piece of the action if a show is perceived to be particularly good.

We made a very good team. She used to call me "Team". After not making further progress with *Moses* due to the fickleness of its writer, we started to produce Shakespeare plays in London fringe venues and at festivals in Germany. Some of them were exceptionally good and deserved a second showing but, as usual, lack of money scuppered our ambition to take things further.

I had the pleasure of meeting Mark Rylance when we produced the first all-female version of *Hamlet*. This was at the London Library, with a journalist who wanted to discuss altered gender versions of Shakespeare. We all know that in Elizabethan times, young men played the female roles, so having an all-female cast in our *Hamlet* was quite an event. Mark Rylance was artistic director of London's Globe Theatre at that time and had an all-male production of another Shakespeare play.

He was memorable for his stillness. He was totally thoughtful and calm, something which is rare amongst actors, as they often seem to be playing a role. It can be an occupational hazard! I once worked with a very fine actor called Cyril Cusack. He too had that quiet but charismatic self-assurance. It was such a lesson for me in acting, as from the read-through he never changed his performance. He appeared completely confident in his interpretation of the part in each scene he was playing. I could not take my eyes off him.

Through my cousin, Joan, I had met a songwriter called David Martin. David had been involved with a 1970s group called Guys and Dolls. He and his writing partners, Geoff Morrow and Chris Arnold, had written songs for many artists including Elvis Presley, Dusty Springfield and Barry Manilow, most famously, "Can't Smile Without you", which had been a huge hit and is still one of the most popular and requested songs of all time. Joan had met David several years before when he had written the early Children in Need theme for BBC TV, and she had been involved in the recording. She reunited with him in 2001 when he brought her sample tapes for a new musical adaptation of Great Expectations. I met him in 2003 after Joan and I decided to produce a showcase performance of this new musical. David had written several very catchy and memorable songs, similar in style to the musical Oliver!, another musical adaptation of the well-read and classical story by Charles Dickens. Joan decided to write the "book" of the show and David added his songs. We put on a shortened version for a showcase at the

Shaw Theatre in Marylebone in a co-production with Richard Price of RPTA, a film, television and stage production company. John Cameron was the arranger and orchestrator of the music. John works across the board, including writing musicals. Jacob Moriarty, now known as Jacob Collier, played young Pip in our showcase. Jacob is now a five-Grammy-Award-winning singer and composer.

We auditioned and found some wonderful singers and actors to play the required roles. The theatre was packed, and the audience loved our musical (many comparing it to *Oliver!*), but as the weeks and months went by, we failed to find a financing producer to take it on. So, like many other potentially great shows, it remains on the shelf waiting to be re-discovered.

One day when visiting David in his Sunningdale flat, he played me some of his old songs. It seemed such a shame that they had not found a home with well-known singers. I had recently been with my old friend Liz to see three short plays at the Old Sorting Office in Barnes, a small fringe theatre. I loved the plays and had the idea of presenting a play with music rather than constructing a straight musical. David and I had a meeting with playwright Carolyn Pertwee. She liked the idea, and we decided to offer "cradle to the grave" story lines. My good friend, Andrew C. Wadsworth, West End star of many musicals, and now a director, directed the show, which we called *A Bowl of Cherries*.

A Bowl of Cherries Poster

Andrew made a very good job of bringing out the humour. Gary Wilmot was our leading man. Gary is a shining example of a great team player and an experienced and inspirational actor, having been a big television star for many years. He is also a great singer.

The musical ran for a month at the Charing Cross Theatre, got some very good reviews and was also nominated for an off-West End award for best ensemble. Sadly, we could not find another theatre or a tour to move the show forward because of the lack of money.

As hard as we tried, we never had quite enough to move it on. It seems to me that theatre projects are often tied up with seasoned theatre impresarios, and smaller companies don't really get a chance to compete. I think it unfair that the National Theatre and the Royal Opera House get a lot of arts funding, leaving less for new young writers and small companies like ours. Thank goodness, though, for the world of fringe theatres, which can offer a stepping stone to well-reviewed productions. In 2018, I got together with Joan again on another new play written by James Hugh Macdonald, a ninety-two-year-old gentleman who had been writing for many years. This was his first play to be staged. It was called *Happy Warriors* and was a play based on the true story of the fractious relationship between Randolph Churchill and Evelyn Waugh when they were billeted together in Yugoslavia during World War Two.

Working on the play brought back many happy memories of previous productions at Upstairs at the Gatehouse Theatre in Highgate. Joan is now a mentor for up-and-coming scriptwriters and is also a judge on the Windsor Fringe Kenneth Branagh Award for New Drama Writing. The Oscar-winning film *The King's Speech* was discovered and developed by Joan. Without her contacts, introductions and efforts, the film would never have been made.

2020 The Pandemic

I felt I had come to the end of my story, as I was happily slowing down, travelling to places that were on my bucket list and enjoying entertaining friends and family in the house during the summer months. Since 1973, I had kept a special place in my heart for Barbados after Derek had made a film there called *The Tamarind Seed* with Julie Andrews and Omar Sharif.

With its beautiful climate and charming people, it is especially nice to visit during the winter months in England. On the 17th March 2020, Johnny and I decided to go and stay at one of our favourite holiday apartments, Maxwell Beach Villas.

Shortly before we left, we heard some disturbing new about a new flu virus that appeared to have started in Wuhan in China, possibly originating in one of those horrible markets where they sell wild animals and cats and dogs for food. There were lots of conspiracy theories at that time too about a manufactured virus created in a Chinese laboratory, but we will probably not find out the truth for a long time.

Our plane was leaving on time at 11 a.m. and flying direct to Grantley Adams Airport in Barbados. Whilst getting calls from friends asking us not to go, we insisted that we would be just as fine there as in the UK, for at that moment in time they only had three confirmed cases of the virus in Barbados. Once we landed and stepped down from the plane, we had to line up to have out temperature taken and then were asked to use a hand sanitiser. No masks were being worn in England at the time we left, but we noticed everyone at the airport wore a mask. There was a huge fine of fifty thousand Barbadian dollars or one year in jail if you broke any rules.

Our two-bedroom holiday apartment was on the ground floor with a lovely terrace overlooking a large garden and pool area with a secure coded gate to the near-deserted beach. It felt like paradise compared to the grey skies and chill wind back in England. Suzanne, the property manager, welcomed us and showed us around. We enjoyed chilled beer on that hot, humid evening as we watched the sun go down. Little did we know that the small apartment would become our home for the next nine weeks.

We formed a crazy golf course round the pool using sun beds and chairs as obstacles, to the amusement of the flat dwellers on the fourth floor, then played cards after lunch. Fortunately, we had great wifi and a TV that had hundreds of stations including Netflix and every decade of music station from the fifties to the nineties. The prime minister of Barbados, Mia Amor Mottley, SC, MP, was a formidable woman, who knew her citizens well and was determined to save as many people as possible. So, she imposed some very strict rules.

The airport for civilians was closed and our plane was not able to return to pick us up. Cruise liners that normally sail in and out of Barbados were refused entry and had to find alternative routes home. During the first week of the imposed lockdown, we were told to stay at home. All shops were closed, even the food stores, which was rather alarming considering we had just two tins of salmon, a dozen eggs, crips, nuts and a little milk.

I was able to find wholesale food producers online to deliver some basics, but we had to order much more than would be sufficient for two people. That didn't matter, however, as we gave away any extras to the remaining staff maintaining the villas. So, we shared out our ten pounds of potatoes, thirty-six eggs, four pineapples and four melons.

Then Suzanne found a chicken farm, so we ordered two whole chickens and several fillets, which was just as well, as we had a large American fridge with a freezer section to fill. One thing we didn't expect was the ban on alcohol.

Having just had a dry February, we now found that we were unable to buy any alcohol again for six weeks. Luckily, we discovered a stash in the bottom of the maid's cupboard. As we didn't have any maid service because of lockdown we "borrowed" (consumed) it then replaced it later. The beautiful beaches were closed to us, but thankfully, as there were only three occupied flats out of ten in the block, they allowed us to use the pool, which was a huge relief.

Despite the friendliness of the people and the beautiful location, the divide between rich and poor is huge. No Barbadian government has been able to sort out the terrible state of the roads and pavements yet. So, walking in Holetown has now become dangerous, with large potholes and gutters forcing you to walk in the road, with local buses and cars coming at you at a manic speed and from all directions.

Many times, you would think you were in a third world country, not in one of the most expensive holiday destinations in the world, particularly when you saw the poor housing the Barbadian people had to live in. Along the coast road, through the west side of the island, live some of the wealthiest people in the world, with restaurants charging well over one hundred pounds for a simple meal. Further inland, ramshackle tin-roofed shacks still exist, which make you wonder where all the money flowing through the island is going to and why it doesn't appear to be going to the native people who live and work there. Maybe the answer lies with the existing federal system.

We were finally able to get a rescue flight home on the 22nd May.

As usual, I ended up sitting next to another of life's eccentrics, Jade Jagger, who was returning home from her holiday home in Mustique. She and her entourage were sitting in the premium economy area, where we were. Business and First Class were taken up with returning crew, as no one was allowed to disembark at that time without being taken to a secure government facility to isolate for ten days.

There was no alcohol on board, only soft drinks and snacks, but as luck would have it, Jade had half a bottle of vodka and I had half a bottle of rum, bought from the only shop open at the airport. We created a bit of a party atmosphere and drank our way through both bottles with diet Cokes as mixers. Johnny was not feeling too well and moved his seat in a disapproving manner. Eventually, a crew member decided to split us up, as we were disturbing the other travellers. We had become firm friends by the end and waved sadly to each other as we went through passport control.

We arrived home in England at the end of May to beautiful weather and just in time to get the garden back together, as it had almost become a wildlife sanctuary with grass and weeds standing three feet high.

Looking back, I think I have been very lucky during my life. I seem to have been in places where things just happened. It is hard to believe that I, an English woman, have experienced two hurricanes, one in Barbados with the memorable Hurricane David. There were seven of us staying in a lovely villa up in the hills on the Sandy Lane Estate, where we had three ladies who looked after us with cooking, cleaning, and washing. The Barbadians all seem to have a great sense of humour and we became very friendly with these ladies. During the evening of the 29th August 1979, Hurricane David swept in. Our ladies gave us a nice dinner then said goodbye and good luck and disappeared down to the coast to shelter in the large church in Holetown. The hurricane hit at about 9 p.m.

The ladies having prepared us with half-open shutters, outdoor furniture in the pool, and a large bottle of rum to keep us going, we sat down to watch the sky and storm coming straight at us from the west coast. The noise was so deafening we could hardly hear ourselves speak. At four in the morning there was a sudden eerie silence, and we could see clear sky. Thank goodness it was over, we thought, but just as we were going back to bed it came back with a vengeance, so we must have been under the eye of the storm for a few minutes.

Eventually, the hurricane passed. We woke up to a brilliant sunny day. Fortunately, there were no deaths, but there was a lot of damage to trees, cars and boats that had been thrown in-land by the waves. Our little family of monkeys that lived in a tropical gully next to us came out to check on us, as we went out to check on them.

Somehow, they knew well before us what was coming, as they were not so visible during that momentous day.

The second hurricane was Hurricane Gustav in September 2008, which followed the worst hurricane in New Orleans' history, Hurricane Katrina. Since that time, the banks of Lake Pontchartrain had been shored up to prevent flooding, so Hurricane Gustav did not cause too much damage. We were staying with our friends, Ronnie and Gardner Kole at the time, in their beautiful house overlooking the bayous in Slidell. We woke to find the house surrounded by water and the roads closed outside. We were isolated and stranded for three days. Ronnie and Gardner had never cooked a meal in their lives but had kept a well-stocked fridge and larder. Johnny and I cooked the meals and, as a treat, Ronnie brought up from their cellar some rare wines they had collected over the years. After dinner, Ronnie, a well-known piano-playing jazz musician, and Johnny would entertain us on the piano with old jazz songs.

SEMI-RETIREMENT

Sarah and I decided to pool our funds and buy some buy-to-let properties. There are many downsides such as call-out for broken boilers, but it keeps me busy with accounts and book-keeping.

Our lives now are full of contentment. We still travel to our flat in Spain and to other holiday resorts, play golf, and keep as active as we can.

We like to look forward to new adventures and have decided to sell this old Windsor house and move into a two-bedroom flat in a retirement village, as we really don't need a large five-bedroom house or a large garden.

All the facilities we require, like restaurants, a pool and gym, can be found in the complex, along with seventy acres of stunning woodland and a lake. It is not far from where we live so will not stop us from seeing our good friends in Windsor and Twickenham.

I have come to the end of my story now and hope my grand-children and great grandchildren will see what life was like growing up in the twentieth century and learn lessons from what they read. The only advice I can give anyone is to live your life to the full as much as you can. Say "yes" to new adventures. Even if you make mistakes don't dwell on them, as you learn from them. Love your friends and family and be kind to people. A kind word said to someone, maybe a stranger, can often lift their mood and make their day, and it costs nothing.

Julie and Johnny

Bibliography:

p. 6, 13, 17–27, 57, 70, 89, 90 (upper), 117, 125: © Julie Samuel, p. 14: © Tina Bailey,
p. 29: © Bill Samuel, p. 45: © Sapphire International Archive, p. 53, 56, 58: © Columbia Films,
p. 65: © Shutterstock Images, p. 72, 82, 85, 90 (bottom right): © Derek Cracknell,
p. 78: © Ray Lonnen, p. 91 (bottom left), 113: © John Stoddart,
p. 104: © Valerie Phillips, p. 126: © Orphan Works Licence

William Foyle and Julie Samuel

HERZ FÜR AUTOREN A HEART FOR AUTHORS À L'ÉCOUTE DES AUTEURS MIA ΚΑΡΔΙΑ ΓΙΑ ΣΥΓ
ATA FÖR FÖRFATTARE UN CORAZÓN POR LOS AUTORES YAZARLARIMIZA GÖNÜL VERELIM S
ORE PER AUTORÍ ET HJERTE FOR FORFATTERE EEN HART VOOR SCHRIJVERS TEMOS OS AU
ZOINKÉRT SERCE DLA AUTORÓW EIN HERZ FÜR AUTOREN A HEART FOR AUTHORS À L'ÉCO
ΚΑΟ ВСЕЙ ДУШОЙ К АВТОРАМ ETT HJÄRTA FÖR FÖRFATTARE Á LA ESCUCHA DE LOS AUT
URS MU KAPΔIÁ ΓΙΑ ΣΥΓΓΡΑΦΕΙΣ UN CUORE PER AUTORI ET HJERTE FOR FORFATTERE EE
ARLARIMIZA GO ERE ZÖINKÉRT SERCE DLA AUTORÓW EIN HERZ F
OR SCHRIJV RTL S O N KAO ВСЕЙ ДУШОЙ К АВТОРАМ ETT HJÄRTA F

The author

Julie Samuel is an accomplished actor, manager
and producer, whose body of work spans the last
seventy decades. A graduate of the renowned
Italia Conti Academy of Theatre Arts, Julie
debuted at the Victoria Palace Theatre at the
age of twelve and went on to perform on stage,
television and the silver screen. Her credits include
roles in Coronation Street, The Day the Earth
Caught Fire and Ferry Cross the Mersey, in which
she played a lead role. In 1985, Julie made a foray
into music management, promoting the singing
career of her daughter, Sarah Cracknell, among
other clients. As a producer, Julie has produced
a number of plays, many of them Shakespeare's
works, and musicals, including the new musical
A Bowl Of Cherries in 2012, which played at the
Charing Cross Theatre in London. Julie has also
produced musical events for the Thames Hospice
care charity, at venues such as Windsor Castle,
Eton College and the Theatre Royal Windsor.

Printed in Great Britain
by Amazon

26126100R00075